DELINEATION
a resource book for architects and illustrators

DELINEATION

a resource book for architects and illustrators
TOBEY · HILDETON

VNR VAN NOSTRAND REINHOLD
———— New York

Copyright © 1992 by Gary Tobey and Nels Hildeton

Library of Congress Catalog Card Number 92-22693
ISBN 0-442-00922-4

All rights reserved. No part of this work covered by the copyright hereon may be reproduced or used in any form or by any means—graphic, electronic, or mechanical, including photocopying, recording, taping, or information storage and retrieval systems—without the written permission of the publisher.

Printed in the United States of America

Van Nostrand Reinhold
115 Fifth Avenue
New York, New York 10003

Chapman & Hall
2-6 Boundary Row
London SE1 8HN, England

Thomas Nelson Australia
102 Dodds Street
South Melbourne 3205
Victoria, Australia

Nelson Canada
1120 Birchmount Road
Scarborough, Ontario
M1K 5G4, Canada

16 15 14 13 12 11 10 9 8 7 6 5 4 3 2 1

Library of Congress Cataloging-in-Publication Data

Tobey, Gary
    Delineation: a resource book for architect and illustrator / Gary Tobey, Nels Hildeton.
       p. cm.
   ISBN 0-442-00922-4
     1. Architectural rendering. I. Hildeton, Nels II. Title.
NA2780 1992
720'.28'4—dc20
                                        92-22693
                                             CIP

CONTENTS

INTRODUCTION — 7

DELINEATION — 9

perspective — 11
TERMINOLOGY — 12
ONE POINT PERSPECTIVE — 14
TWO POINT PERSPECTIVE — 16

composition — 19
POINT OF VIEW — 20
ARRANGEMENT OF ENTOURAGE — 26
USE OF TONAL VALUES — 32
FOREGROUND · MIDDLEGROUND · BACKGROUND — 36

using the pencil — 41
MATERIALS — 42
NATURAL TEXTURES — 46
SHADE AND SHADOW — 50

site plans and elevations — 57
SITE PLAN & ELEVATION EMBELLISHMENT — 58

TRACING FILE — 63

vegetation — 65

vehicles — 129

people — 189

INTRODUCTION

ARCHITECTURAL DELINEATION CAN BE LEARNED AND PERFECTED THROUGH THE LOGICAL STEPS PRESENTED WITHIN THIS BOOK. IT FOCUSES ON THE ESSENTIALS OF A GOOD RENDERING AND BASES ITSELF ON A SINGLE "STYLE" OF ILLUSTRATION, THAT OF THE AUTHORS.

THE ESSENTIALS OF RENDERING ARE: COMPOSITION, PERSPECTIVE, SHADE, SHADOW, AND TEXTURE. A SUCCESSFUL RENDERING WILL BE A WELL COMPOSED PATTERN OF DARKS AND LIGHTS ACCOMPANIED BY TEXTURAL VARIATION, ALL WITHIN A FRAMEWORK OF A CORRECT PERSPECTIVE. BOTH THOSE WHO CONSTRUCT PERSPECTIVES BY HAND AND THOSE WHO GENERATE A WIRE FRAME ON A COMPUTER WILL FIND THE ARTISTIC GUIDELINES TO TRANSFORM BARE-BONES PERSPECTIVES INTO HANDSOME RENDERINGS.

MANY ARCHITECTS AND ILLUSTRATORS FIND IT DIFFICULT TO DRAW TREES, CARS, AND PEOPLE; THEREFORE, WE HAVE DEVOTED A LARGE PORTION OF THIS BOOK TO A TRACING FILE OF THESE ITEMS WHICH WILL ADD A LARGE MEASURE OF REALISM TO YOUR RENDERING. THE TRACING FILE WILL SAVE IMMEASURABLE TIME AND ALLOW YOU TO POSITION THE ITEMS TRACED SO THAT THE BEST POSSIBLE COMPOSITION IS ACHIEVED. FEEL FREE TO ENLARGE, REDUCE, OR MODIFY THE ITEMS WITHIN THIS TRACING FILE TO SUIT YOUR NEEDS. WITH CONTINUED USE OF THIS FILE, YOU WILL DEVELOP A SELF-CONFIDENCE AND PERSONAL STYLE THAT WILL BECOME YOUR OWN TRADEMARK.

DELINEATION

perspective

terminology

THE TERMS DEFINED HERE ARE USED IN THE INSTRUCTIONS FOR CONSTRUCTING PERSPECTIVE DRAWINGS, WHICH ARE ON THE FOLLOWING PAGES.

1. THE STATION POINT, **SP**, LOCATES THE POSITION OF THE VIEWER ON THE PLAN. IT IS THE POINT OF VIEW FROM WHICH WE WILL SEE THE BUILDING.

2. A VISUAL RAY, **VR**, IS A LINE RADIATING FROM THE STATION POINT TO A POINT ON THE PLAN WHICH THE VIEWER WISHES TO SEE IN THE PERSPECTIVE DRAWING.

3. THE PICTURE PLANE, **PP**, IS THE PLANE ONTO WHICH THE BUILDING IS PROJECTED BY MEANS OF THE VISUAL RAYS.

4. THE CENTRAL VISUAL RAY, **CVR**, IS THE CENTRAL AXIS WITHIN THE VIEWERS FIELD OF VISION AND IT IS ALWAYS PERPENDICULAR TO THE PICTURE PLANE.

5. THE GROUND LINE, **GL**, LIES AT THE BASE OF THE BUILDING AND AT A POINT WHERE THE PICTURE PLANE INTERSECTS THE BUILDING.

6. THE HORIZON LINE, **HL**, IS THE "EYE LEVEL" LINE TO WHICH ALL HORIZONTAL LINES IN PERSPECTIVE CONVERGE.

7. THE VANISHING POINT, **VP**, IS A POINT TO WHICH PARALLEL LINES CONVERGE. THERE IS AT LEAST ONE IN A PERSPECTIVE DRAWING AND FREQUENTLY MORE.

8. THE VERTICAL MEASURE LINE, **VML**, IS THE VERTICAL LINE ALONG WHICH WE MEASURE THE HEIGHTS OF VARIOUS ELEMENTS OF THE BUILDING. IT IS ALWAYS LOCATED ON THE PICTURE PLANE AND IS THE ONLY TRUE-SCALE LINE IN THE PERSPECTIVE DRAWING.

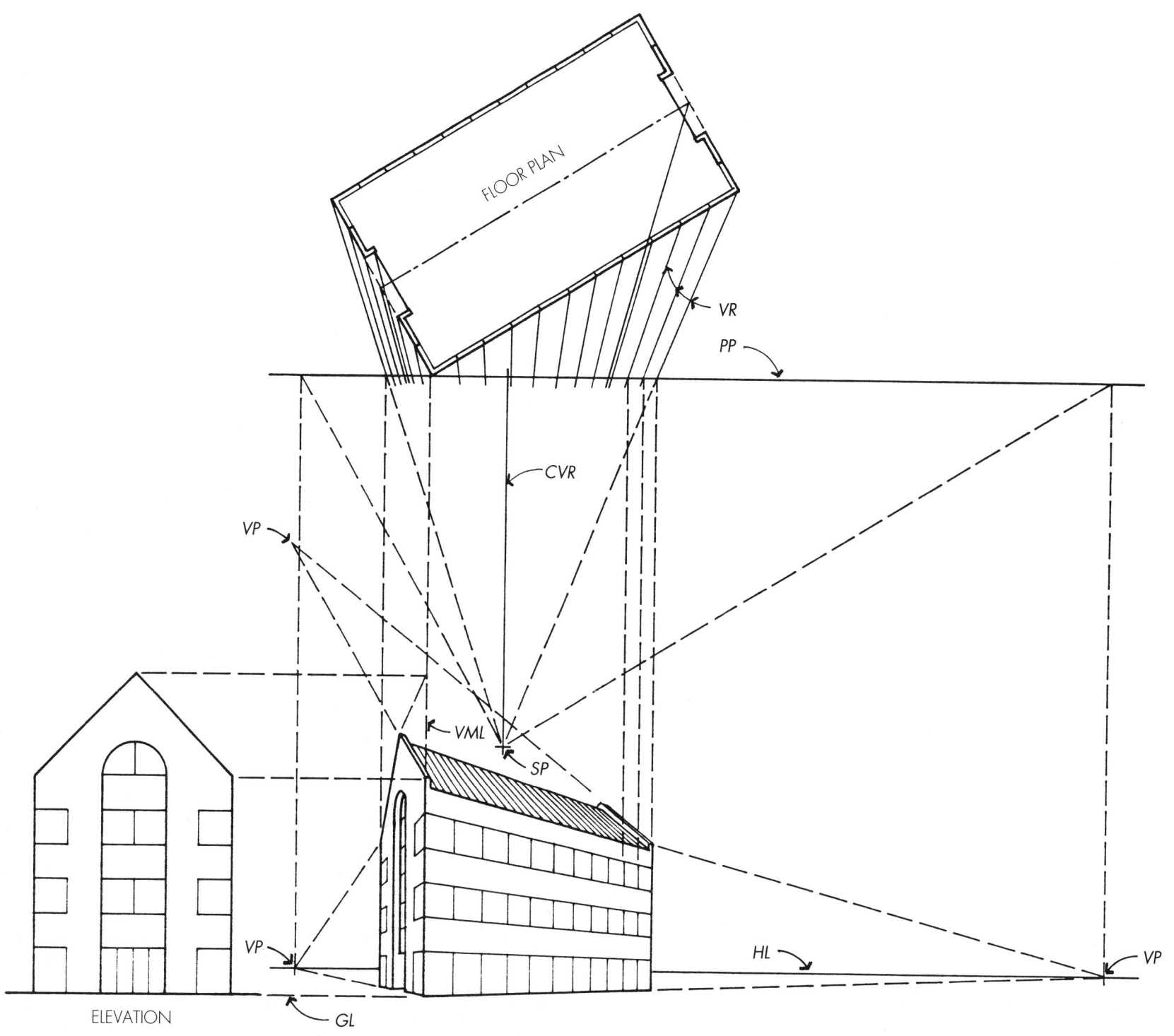

one point perspective

1. SET THE PLAN PARALLEL TO YOUR TEE SQUARE.

2. DRAW THE PICTURE PLANE, **PP**, ON THE FACE OF THE BUILDING.

3. DRAW THE CENTRAL VISUAL RAY, **CVR**, PERPENDICULAR TO THE PICTURE PLANE AT A POSITION APPROXIMATELY DISSECTING THE PLAN IN HALF.

4. SET THE STATION POINT, **SP**, AT THE DESIRED DISTANCE FROM THE BUILDING.

5. INSTALL A PUSH PIN AT **SP** AND EXTEND LINES FROM THE NEAR CORNERS AND COLUMNS OF THE BUILDING TO THE PICTURE PLANE.

6. SET THE BUILDING'S ELEVATION BELOW AND OFF TO ONE SIDE.

7. DRAW THE HORIZON LINE 5 FEET ABOVE GRADE.

8. DROP THE **CVR** DOWN TO INTERSECT **HL**. THIS INTERSECTION IS THE VANISHING POINT. THE VANISHING POINT FOR A ONE POINT PERSPECTIVE IS ALWAYS AT THE INTERSECTION OF THE CENTRAL VISUAL RAY AND THE PICTURE PLANE.

9. PROJECT HORIZONTAL LINES FROM THE ELEVATION TO DRAW THE FACE OF THE BUILDING WHICH LIES ON THE PICTURE PLANE. THE FACE IS DRAWN TO SCALE BECAUSE ANYTHING FALLING ON THE **PP** IS ALWAYS TO SCALE.

10. PROJECT VERTICAL LINES DOWN FROM THE INTERSECTIONS OF THE **VR**'S AND **PP**.

11. USING THE VANISHING POINT, DRAW HORIZONTAL LINES FORWARD TO THE NEAR CORNERS, AND THEN ACROSS THE NEAR WALLS.

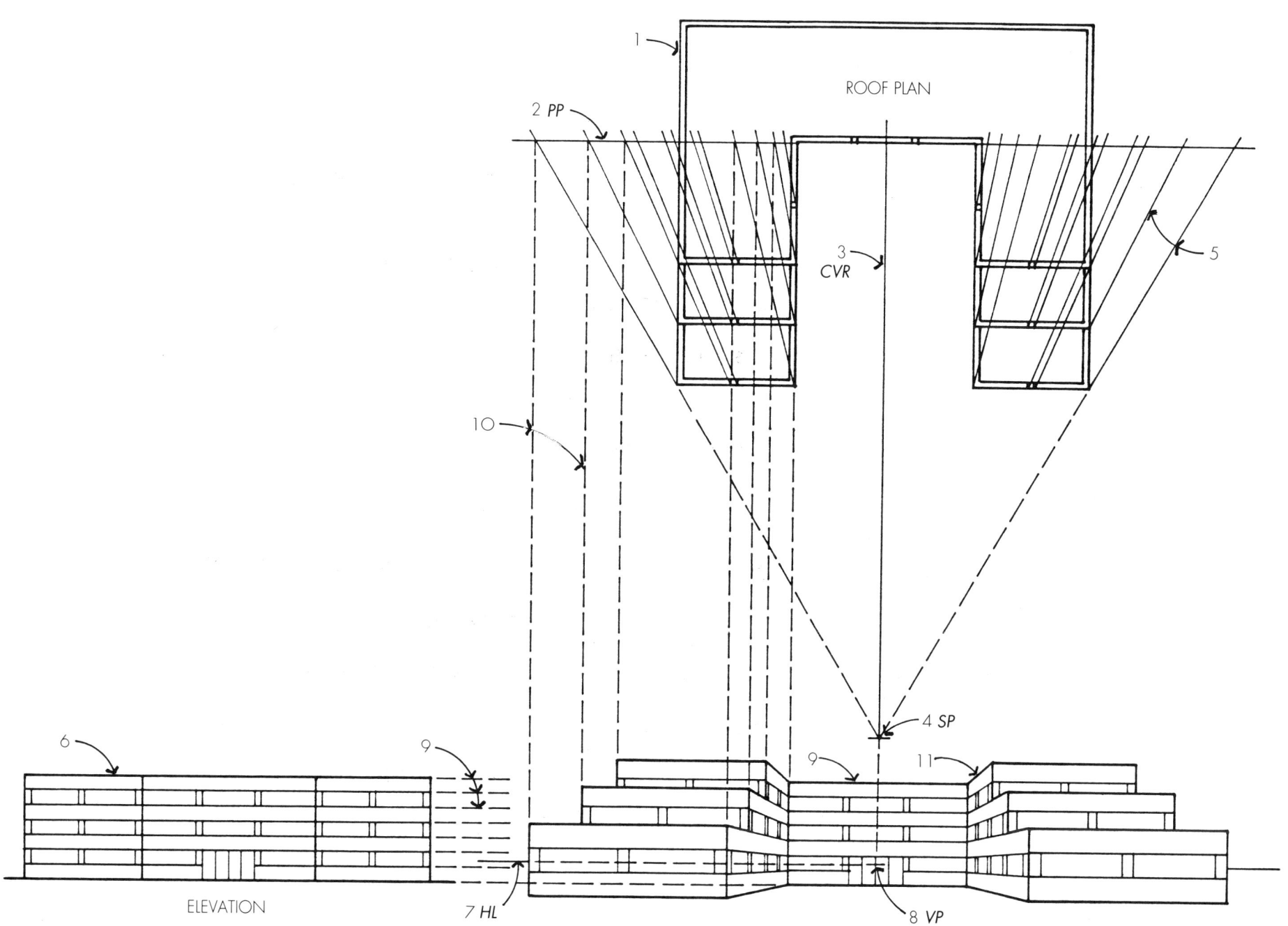

two point perspective

SELECT A BUILDING PLAN WHICH IS RECTANGULAR AND FOLLOW THIS PROCEDURE STEP BY STEP TO GENERATE A PERSPECTIVE DRAWING.

1. SET THE PLAN AT THE DESIRED ANGLE; IN THIS CASE IT IS 30 DEGREES.
2. DRAW THE PICTURE PLANE, *PP*, THROUGH THE NEAR CORNER OF THE PLAN.
3. DRAW THE CENTRAL VISUAL RAY, *CVR*, PERPENDICULAR TO THE PICTURE PLANE AT A POSITION APPROXIMATELY DISSECTING THE PLAN IN HALF.
4. SET THE STATION POINT, *SP*, AT THE DESIRED DISTANCE FROM THE BUILDING.
5. INSTALL A PUSH PIN AT *SP* AND EXTEND LINES FROM THE CORNERS OF THE BUILDING, FROM THE WINDOW MULLIONS AND ENDS OF THE ROOF RIDGE TO *PP*.
6. EXTEND LINES, WHICH ARE PARALLEL TO THE PLAN, FROM *SP* TO *PP*.
7. DRAW THE HORIZON LINE, *HL*, AT A CONVENIENT SPOT BELOW THE PICTURE PLANE.
8. PROJECT FROM THE INTERSECTIONS OF *PP* AND THE NUMBER SIX LINES DOWN TO *HL*, THUS ESTABLISHING THE VANISHING POINTS, *VP*.
9. DRAW THE VERTICAL MEASURE DOWN FROM THE INTERSECTION OF *PP* AND THE NEAR CORNER OF THE BUILDING.
10. PLACE THE ELEVATION OF THE BUILDING WITH THE FIRST FLOOR 5 FEET BELOW THE HORIZON LINE, WHICH WILL GENERATE A NORMAL GROUND LEVEL PERSPECTIVE. THE ELEVATION MUST BE AT THE SAME SCALE AS THE PLAN.
11. PROJECT THE HEIGHTS OF THE VARIOUS ELEMENTS OF THE BUILDING OVER TO THE *VML*. MAKE TICK MARKS ON THE *VML*.
12. INSTALL PUSH PINS IN THE *VP'S* AND DRAW LINES FROM THE TICK MARKS ON THE *VML* TO THE *VIP'S*, THUS PRODUCING HORIZONTAL LINES IN PERSPECTIVE.
13. PROJECT VERTICAL LINES DOWN FROM WHERE THE VISUAL RAYS, *VR*, INTERSECT THE PICTURE PLANE.
14. TO LOCATE THE ROOF RIDGE IN PERSPECTIVE, PROJECT A LINE TO THE VANISHING POINT ON THE LEFT AND FROM WHERE THIS LINE INTERSECTS THE VISUAL RAY FROM ABOVE, DRAW A LINE TO THE VANISHING POINT ON THE RIGHT.
15. DRAW THE GABLE BY CONNECTING THE TOP CORNERS OF THE BUILDING WITH THE ENDS OF THE RIDGE.

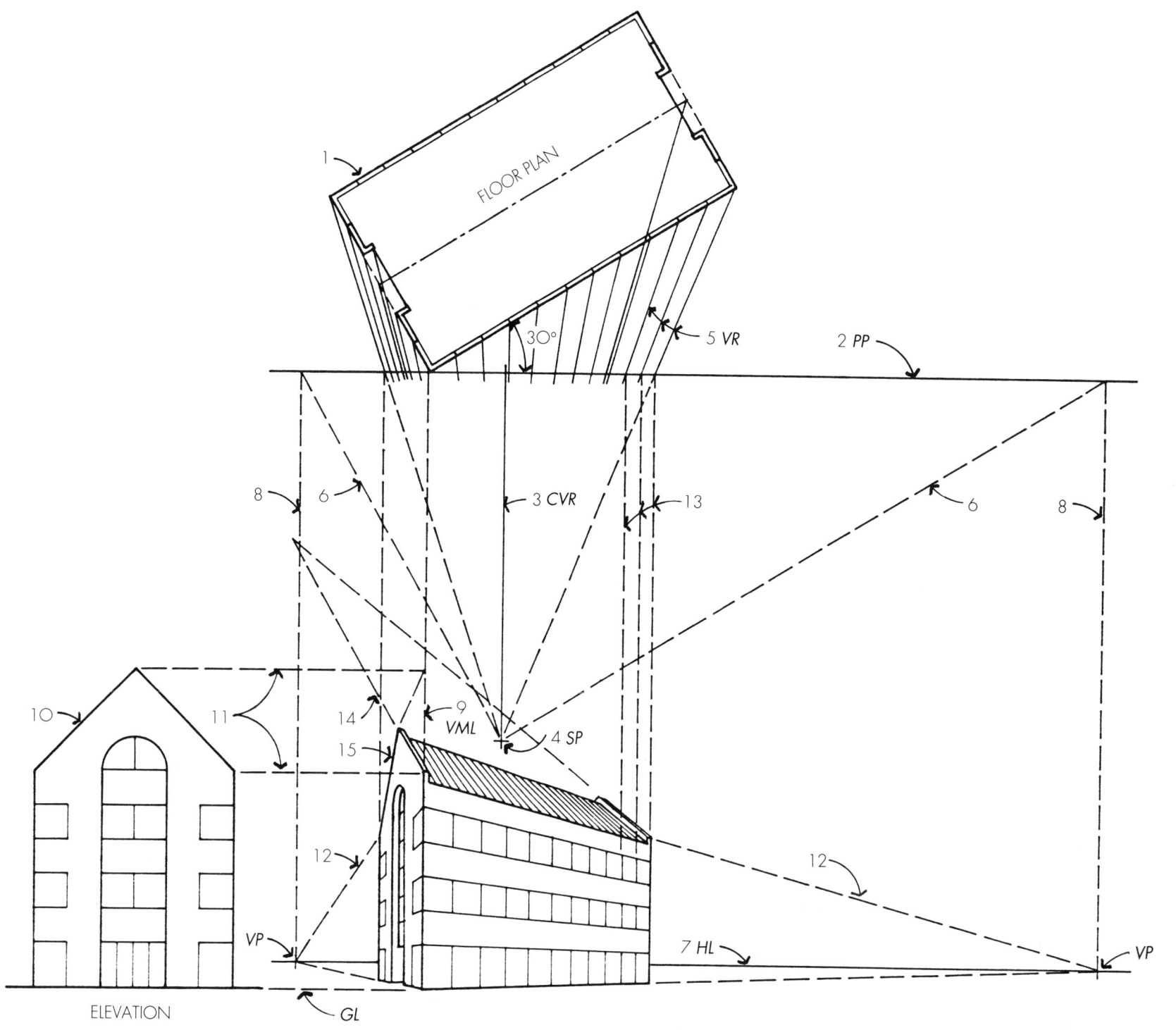

composition

point of view

Deciding on a point of view or station point, as it is known to delineators, is really just a matter of common sense, as no formal procedure exists.

A likely location for a station point might be found by studying the site plan and seeing where most people will be viewing the project: from a heavily traveled intersection, a busy boulevard, or simply a pedestrian walkway. In most cases the best point of view will be evident.

We usually want to see a building from a position standing on the ground, because this is where most people will see the building once it is built. Keep in mind your eye level is between 4 and 5 feet above grade.

At times, a bird's eye view is the best way to view a more complicated building or multiple buildings within a project. This is not a natural viewing angle unless the project is located in a depression that is lower than the streets around it, or we are viewing the project from a neighboring high rise. Likewise, a building or complex that is located on a knoll might best be seen from a worm's eye view. Each building, along with its site, has individual characteristics which will, in the final analysis, dictate from where it should be viewed. Let's face it, your client may simply tell you what view they want.

In any event, study the site and the building's characteristics carefully. Maybe even do a few freehand sketches before investing a lot of time in your finished rendering.

arrangement of entourage

WHEN PROPERLY ARRANGED, THE SURROUNDING ENVIRONMENT OR ENTOURAGE WILL CREATE DEPTH, GIVE SCALE, ADD DRAMA AND PLACE YOUR SUBJECT IN ITS INTENDED CONTEXT. BY CHOOSING THE TYPE OF TREES AND BACKGROUND THAT ALREADY EXISTS ON OR NEAR THE SITE, YOU WILL IMPART AN APPEARANCE OF REALITY TO YOUR RENDERING.

ARRANGEMENT OF ENTOURAGE IS NOT A PROCESS WITH A FORMULA; RATHER, IT IS AN ADVENTURE GUIDED BY ARTISTIC INSTINCTS. SOME OF US INHERENTLY POSSESS THE INSTINCTS FOR GOOD COMPOSITION, WHILE THE REST OF US MUST DEVELOP THEM THROUGH PRACTICE. WE RECOMMEND IN EITHER CASE TO ALWAYS MAKE A NUMBER OF OVERLAYS SHOWING THE ENTOURAGE IN DIFFERENT CONFIGURATIONS UNTIL THE RIGHT COMPOSITION COMES ALONG.

TWO PRINCIPLES HAVE GUIDED US DURING OUR YEARS OF COMPOSING RENDERINGS. ONE IS TO MAINTAIN VISUAL BALANCE IN THE COMPOSITION AND THE OTHER IS TO BE SURE THAT THE ENTOURAGE DOES NOT COMPETE WITH THE PRIMARY SUBJECT ITSELF. TO MAINTAIN BALANCE, DISTRIBUTE ELEMENTS OF ENTOURAGE EVENLY THROUGHOUT THE COMPOSITION AND WHEN PLACING A LARGE ELEMENT ON THE LEFT, BALANCE IT ON THE RIGHT WITH SOMETHING OF EQUAL IMPACT BUT NOT NECESSARILY EQUAL SIZE. TO AVOID COMPETING WITH THE MAIN SUBJECT NEVER PLACE A LARGE FOREGROUND ELEMENT IN THE CENTER OF YOUR COMPOSITION. INSTEAD, TRY PLACING IT TO ONE SIDE, DRAWING ONLY PART OF IT. THIS WAY, THE LARGE OBJECT IN THE FOREGROUND WON'T COMMAND TOO MUCH ATTENTION, BUT WILL ENHANCE THE DEPTH AND DRAMA.

WHILE THESE PRINCIPLES ARE NOT HARD AND FAST, TWO RULES ARE: (1) ALL ELEMENTS OF ENTOURAGE MUST BE THE CORRECT SIZE FOR WHERE THEY OCCUR IN THE PERSPECTIVE, AND (2) THE ELEMENTS MUST BE IN CORRECT PERSPECTIVE AND, THEREFORE, OBJECTS SUCH AS CARS AND FURNITURE SHOULD ALWAYS BE PARALLEL TO THE GROUND OR FLOOR.

ON THE FOLLOWING PAGES WE SHOW EXAMPLES OF HOW PERSPECTIVE DRAWINGS CAN BE EMBELLISHED WITH ENTOURAGE USING THESE RULES AND PRINCIPLES.

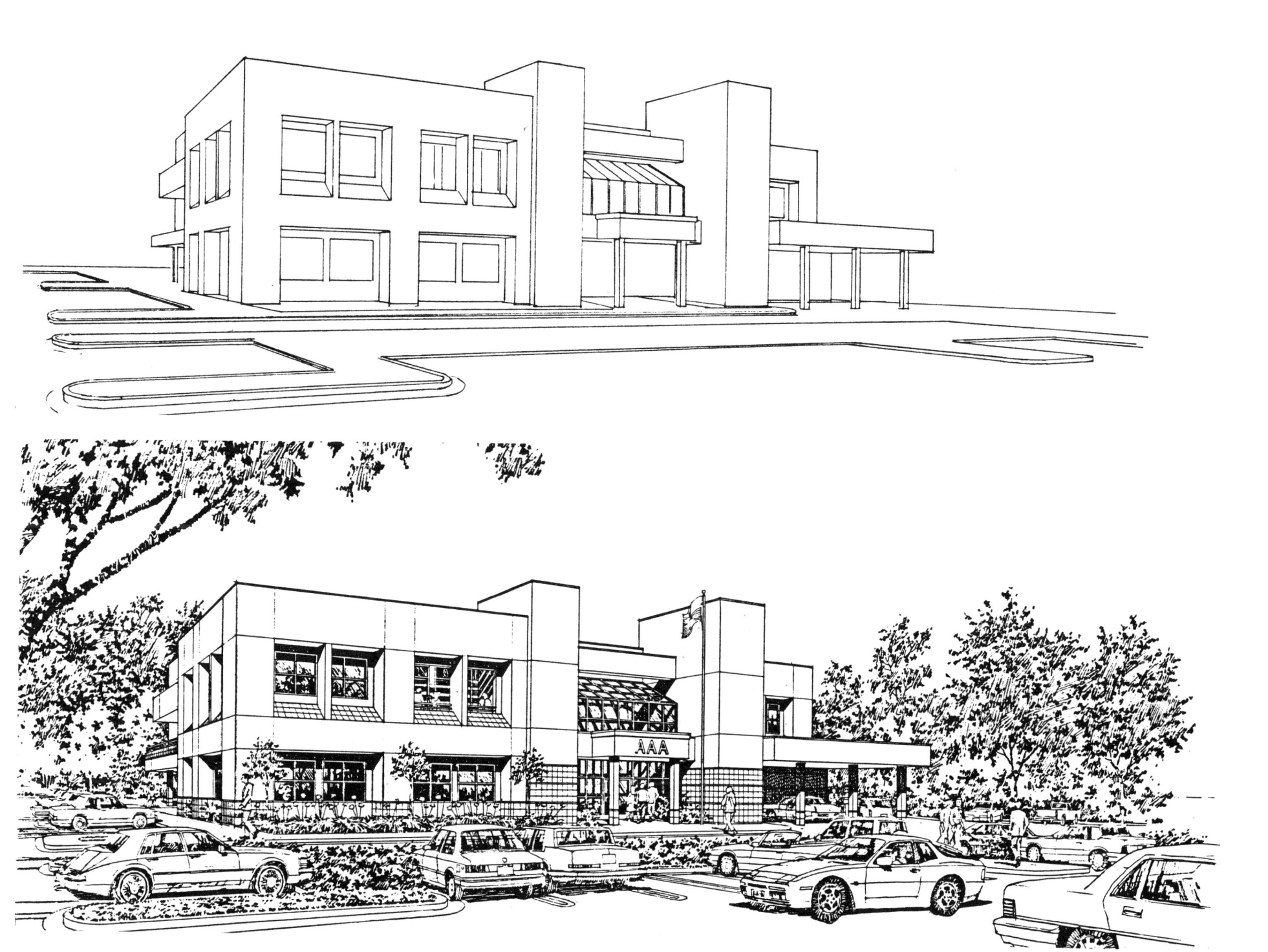

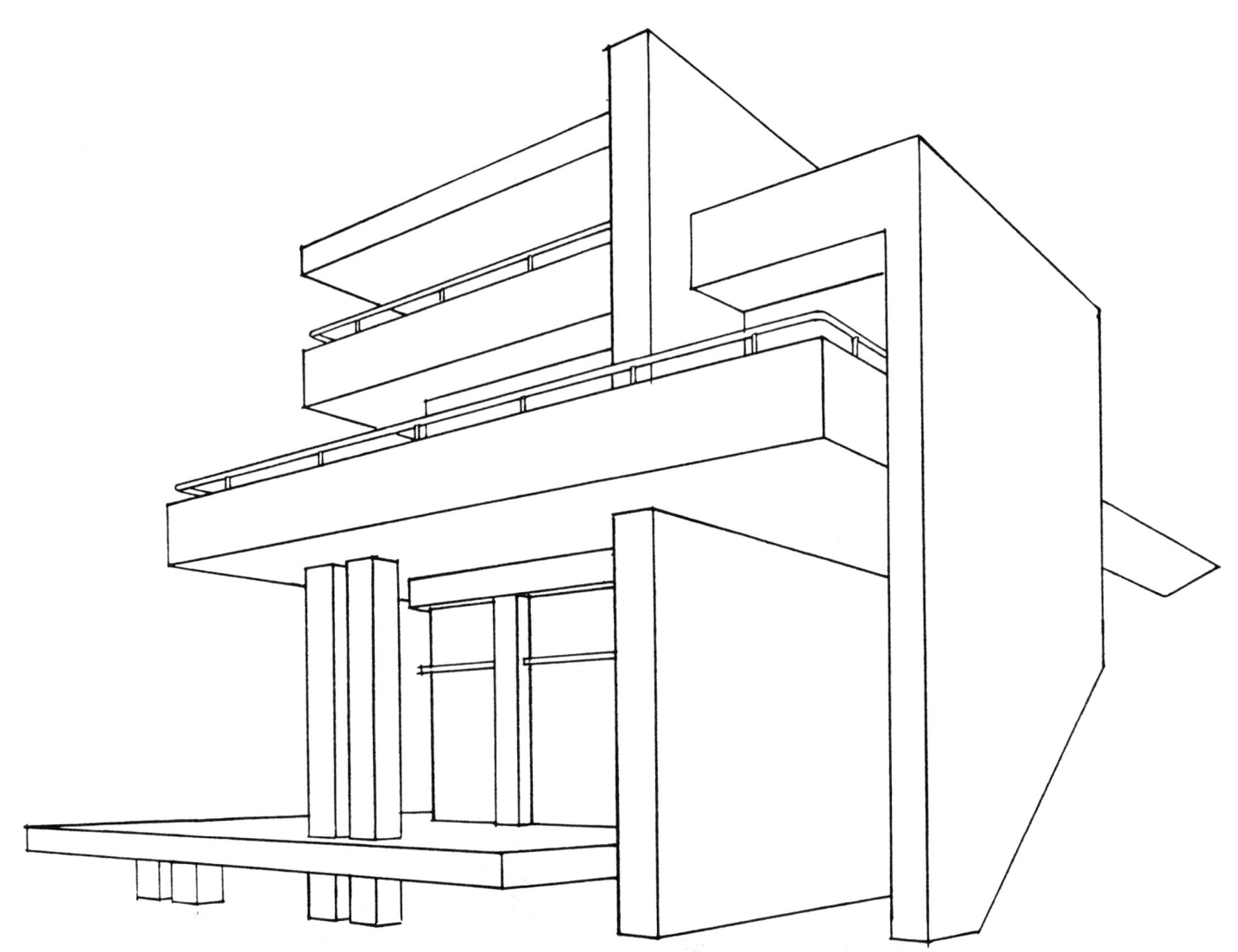

use of tonal values

SHADE AND SHADOW ARE TONES WHICH DEFINE THE FORM OF AN OBJECT AND THE TEXTURE DESCRIBES ITS SURFACE. APPLYING TONAL VALUES IS TIME-CONSUMING AND, FOR BEGINNERS, CAN BE FRUSTRATING, BUT SOME PERSEVERANCE HERE WILL BE REWARDING. THE DELINEATIONS IN THIS BOOK ARE PENCIL LINE DRAWINGS TO WHICH SHADE, SHADOW AND TEXTURE HAVE BEEN APPLIED. TREES AND SHRUBS ARE AN EXCEPTION BECAUSE HERE THE TEXTURE IS THE DEFINING EDGE.

IN OUR ILLUSTRATIONS TONES ARE PRODUCED BY SIMPLY DRAWING LINES. TO ACHIEVE DARK TONES WE SPACE THE PENCIL STROKES CLOSE TOGETHER AND APPLY HEAVY PRESSURE. FOR LIGHTER TONES WE SPACE THE LINES FARTHER APART OR REDUCE THE PRESSURE ON THE PENCIL.

WE HAVE FOUND THAT BLACK, DARK GREY, LIGHT GREY AND WHITE WILL BE ENOUGH TONES TO WORK WITH IN THE AVERAGE RENDERING. BLACK IS RESERVED MOSTLY FOR BUILDING AND ENTOURAGE SHADOWS AS WELL AS REFLECTIONS IN WINDOWS. USE THE DARK GREY AND LIGHT GREY ON THE SHADED SURFACES OF THE BUILDING AND ENTOURAGE. AFTER THESE TONES HAVE BEEN APPLIED, POSITIVE AND NEGATIVE WHITE SPACE EMERGE AND IT IS THESE CONTRASTS WHICH GIVE OUR RENDERING BRILLIANCE.

BEGINNERS CAN CREATE A SUCCESSFUL RENDERING BY RESTRICTING THE USE OF TONE TO THE BUILDING AND SELECTED ELEMENTS IN THE FOREGROUND AND BACKGROUND. IT IS NOT NECESSARY TO SHADE, SHADOW AND TEXTURE THE ENTIRE TREE OR CAR. TEXTURE ON THE SHADED SIDE OF A TREE, BOLD SHADOW AT THE BOTTOM OF FOLIAGE AND A BLACK SHADOW ON THE GROUND SAY TREE. SHADOW UNDER A CAR AND SHADE ON TIRES AND WHEEL WELLS IS SUFFICIENT. ONCE YOUR CONFIDENCE IS DEVELOPED, WE ENCOURAGE YOU TO USE A VARIETY OF TONES ON THE ELEMENTS TAKEN FROM THE TRACING FILE.

foreground · middleground · background

WHEN LOOKING AT AN ARCHITECTURAL ILLUSTRATION WE THINK OF THE AREA CLOSEST TO US AS FOREGROUND, THE NEXT AREA AS MIDDLEGROUND AND BEHIND THAT, AS FAR AS THE EYE CAN SEE, AS BACKGROUND.

MOST FREQUENTLY OUR PRIMARY SUBJECT, THE BUILDING, IS LOCATED IN THE MIDDLEGROUND; THEREFORE, THE FOREGROUND AND BACKGROUND PLAY A SUPPORTING ROLE IN OUR COMPOSITION. CARE MUST BE TAKEN TO INSURE THAT THE FOREGROUND AND BACKGROUND COMPLIMENT AND ENHANCE THE BUILDING. ELEMENTS OF THE FOREGROUND SUCH AS ROADS, PARKING LOTS AND LAWNS SHOULD BE SHADED AND TEXTURED SO THAT THE EYE OF THE VIEWER IS LED TO THE BUILDING. TREES AND SUPPORTING OBJECTS IN THE FOREGROUND SHOULD ACT AS A FRAME AROUND THE BUILDING, POSSIBLY SHRUBS AT THE BASE, TREES AT THE SIDES AND BRANCHES OVERHEAD. WHEN THERE ARE NO TREES OR LANDSCAPING IN THE FOREGROUND, SHADOWS FROM CLOUDS OR OTHER BUILDINGS AS WELL AS CARS AND PEOPLE CAN BE INTRODUCED TO FRAME THE COMPOSITION.

IN RENDERINGS OF LIGHT COLORED BUILDINGS, ELEMENTS OF THE BACKGROUND CAN BE MADE DARKER, CAUSING THE BUILDINGS TO STAND OUT BY CONTRAST. CONVERSELY, DARKER BUILDINGS BENEFIT FROM LIGHTER BACKGROUNDS.

ILLUSTRATE ELEMENTS IN THE FOREGROUND WITH MORE DETAIL AND BOLD LINE WEIGHT. BECAUSE OUR PERCEPTION OF DISTANT OBJECTS IS LESS, DELINEATE DISTANT OBJECTS WITH LESS DETAIL AND STRENGTH. THIS ENHANCES THE DEPTH OF THE RENDERING AND IT IS THE WAY YOUR EYE PERCEIVES OBJECTS, NEAR AND FAR, IN NATURE.

materials

ASIDE FROM THE FORM OF THE BUILDING, THE MATERIALS ON ITS SURFACES ARE WHAT WE SEE AS ACTUALLY REPRESENTING THE BUILDING IN OUR RENDERINGS. THE BUILDING'S MATERIALS SHOULD BE FAITHFULLY DELINEATED.

RENDERING MATERIALS ON BUILDINGS AT A DISTANCE REQUIRES RESTRAINT AND A LIGHT TOUCH, BECAUSE WE WANT THE MATERIALS TO BE AS SUBTLE AS THEY ARE IN REAL LIFE. BRICK, STONE, SIDING, SHINGLES AND OTHER MATERIALS WHICH CREATE PATTERNS, SHOULD BE DRAWN LIGHTER AND WITH LESS DETAIL THAN THE BUILDING ITSELF.

SMOOTH, DULL FINISHES LIKE METAL, CONCRETE AND STUCCO CAN BE LEFT PLAIN IN MOST CASES FOR THE BEST RESULTS. KEEP IN MIND MATERIALS ON BUILDINGS CLOSER TO THE VIEWER DISPLAY MORE DETAIL AND, THEREFORE, WE DRAW THE GRAIN IN THE WOOD, THE TEXTURE IN STONE AND THE JOINTS IN BRICK. DRAW THESE MATERIALS DARKER THAN THOSE AT A DISTANCE.

RENDERING GLASS SCARES MANY PEOPLE, PROBABLY BECAUSE IT IS SIMULTANEOUSLY TRANSPARENT AND REFLECTIVE. IN MOST INSTANCES THE REFLECTIONS OF TREES, BUILDINGS AND SKY DOMINATE WHAT WE SEE IN GLASS. KEEP YOUR TASK SIMPLE BY DRAWING REFLECTIONS ONLY. IF YOU WANT TO ILLUSTRATE TRANSPARENCY IT IS NOT NECESSARY TO DRAW THE ENTIRE CONTENTS OF A ROOM. ON LOWER FLOORS DRAW DARK SILHOUETTES OF OBJECTS AND PEOPLE AND ON UPPER FLOORS INDICATE LIGHT FIXTURES ON THE CEILINGS. ON TALL BUILDINGS GRADUATE THE SHADING OF GLASS FROM DARK AT THE BOTTOM TO LIGHT AT THE TOP.

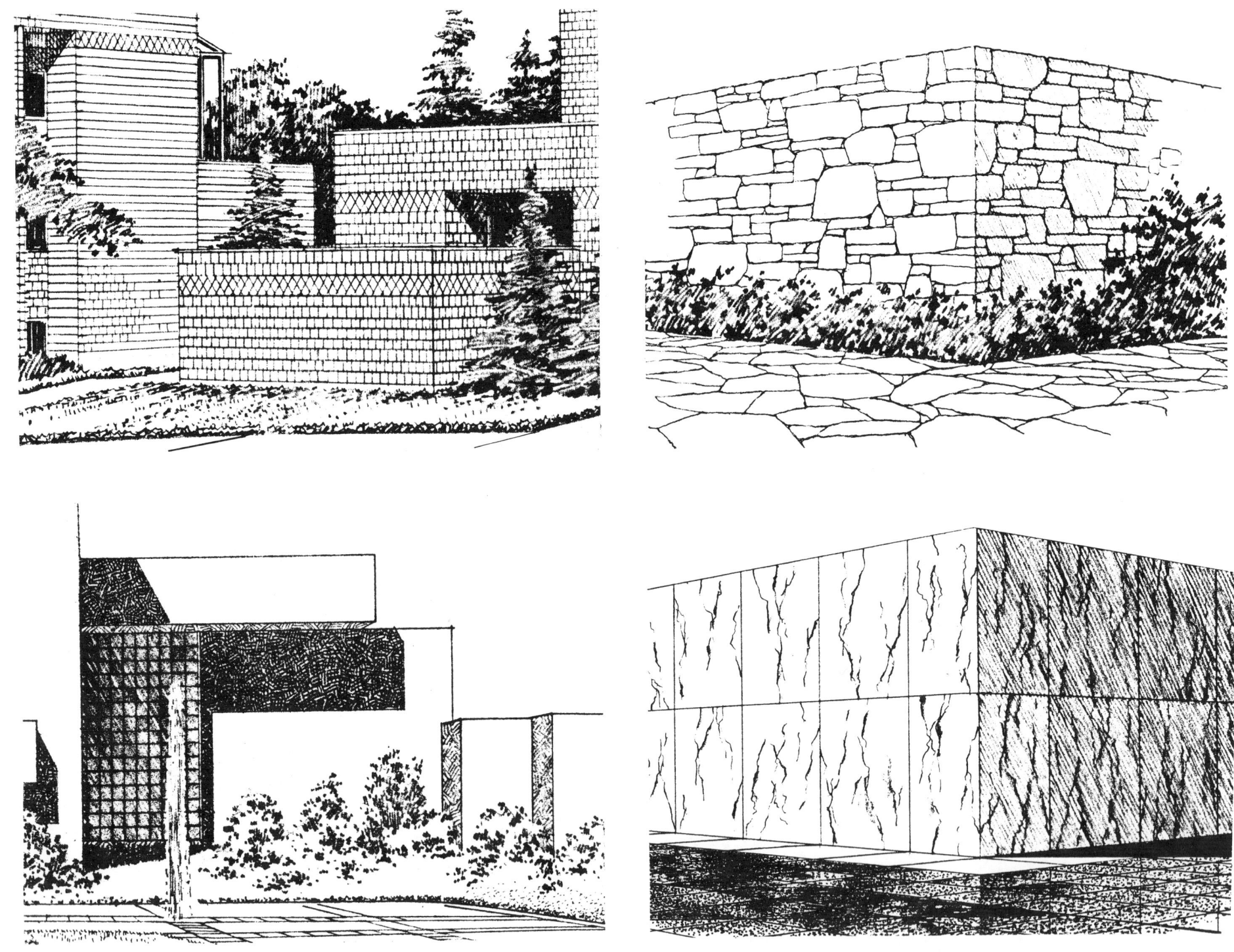

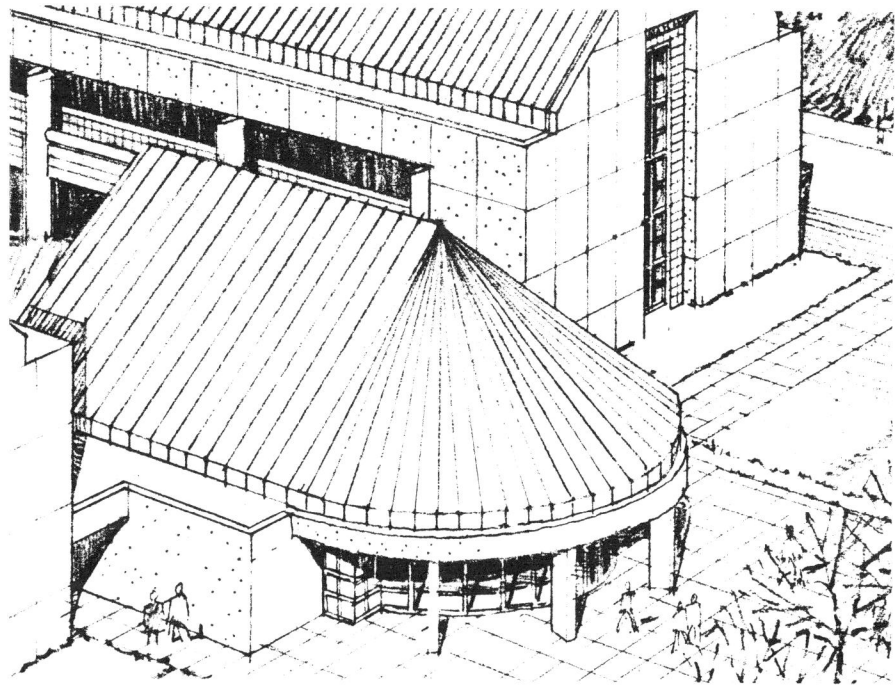

natural textures

Natural textures most often are a repetitive pattern with each repetition somewhat varied from the other. When we look at rough water, the waves are all approximately the same size and shape but not quite. Similarly the overall texture of foliage on trees and shrubs is repetitious with slight variation from area to area. To represent foliage, use short hatched lines, varying the length and direction. Let the strokes overlap to create darker areas, and leave light areas where foliage is catching the sun. Go back and add darks at the bottom to indicate shade. Ground cover, such as ivy, is rendered with an overall texture, keeping the strokes more or less parallel to the ground plane. To delineate lawns, use a few lines that follow the ground plane and add some short strokes in the foreground to indicate the texture of grass. Doing this will imply that the large area left blank is lawn.

In nature, rocks occur in regular and irregular patterns and may or may not vary in size. You will have to decide which pattern and size suit you. They can be illustrated easiest with lines that fluctuate dark to light, and then add textured tone to the shaded side.

Delineating water can be difficult. The key is to draw very little and let the rest be implied, just as we do with the lawns. Calm water is rendered with a few wavy lines and rough water with patches of texture in the shape of waves. The coup de gras is to add a reflection of what is on the shoreline; make a reverse print of what you have drawn on the shore and trace it upside down in the water.

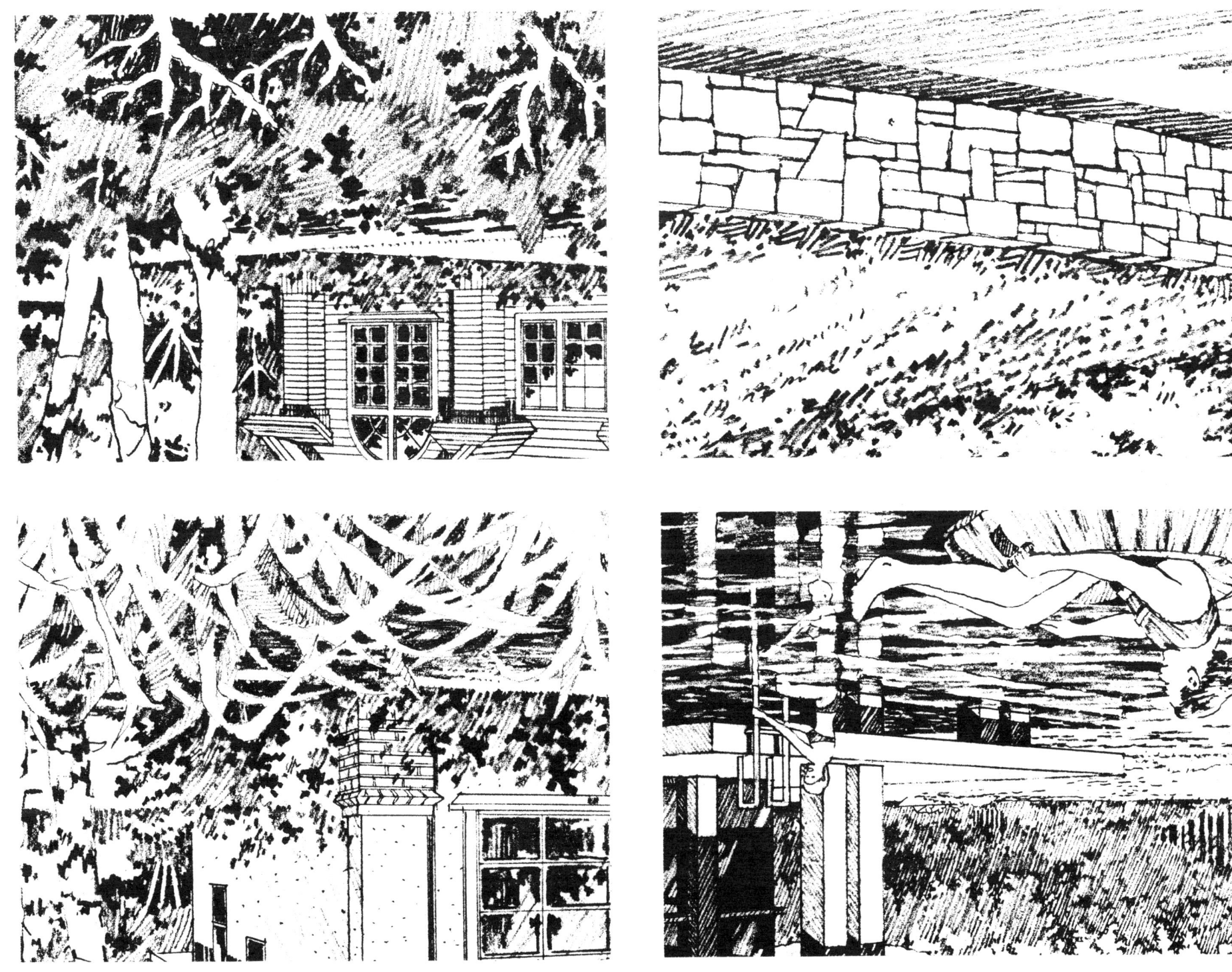

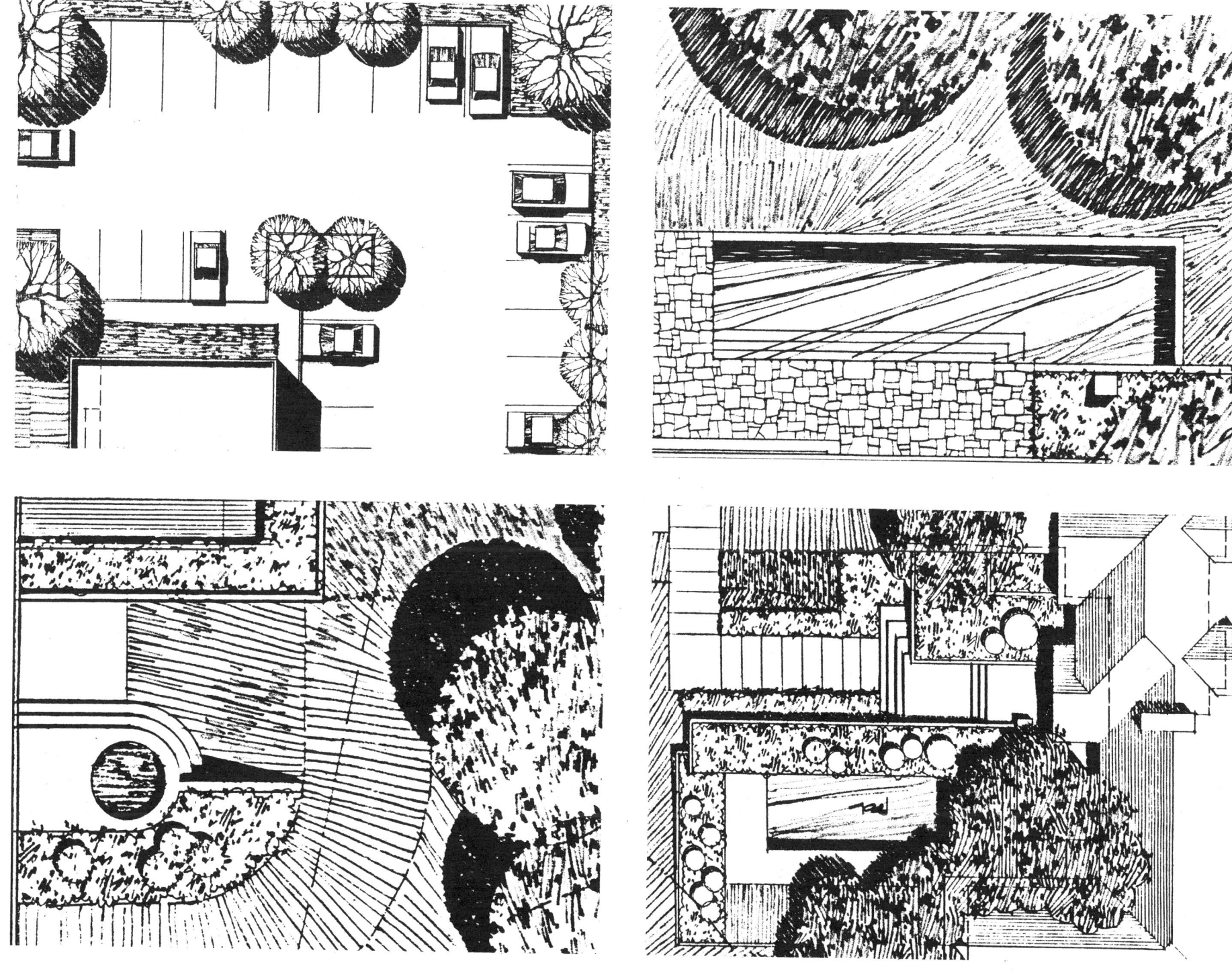

shade and shadow

SHADE IS A SURFACE WHICH DOES NOT RECEIVE DIRECT LIGHT. SHADOW IS THE DARK AREA CAST OR PROJECTED ONTO A LIGHTED SURFACE BY A SHADED AREA. WE USE THE WORD "PROJECTED," IN A DRAWING SENSE BECAUSE, IN REALITY, SHADOWS ARE NOT PROJECTED; THEY ARE AREAS OF DARKNESS CAUSED BY THE SUNLIGHT BEING BLOCKED BY SOME OBJECT. IT IS THE EDGES OF THE SHADED AREA, WHEN PROJECTED ONTO A LIGHTED SURFACE, THAT DEFINE THE PERIMETER OF A SHADOW. SHADE RECEIVES REFLECTED LIGHT FROM SURROUNDING SURFACES, WHILE SHADOW RECEIVES VERY LITTLE. CONSEQUENTLY, SHADOW IS MUCH DARKER THAN SHADE IN A RENDERING.

LEARNING TO CONSTRUCT ALL THE POSSIBLE VARIATIONS OF DIFFERENT SHAPES AND SUN ANGLES IS A TEDIOUS AFFAIR. WE TAKE A SIMPLE APPROACH TO SHADE AND SHADOW AND UNLESS YOU ARE SCIENTIFICALLY INCLINED, WE RECOMMEND THAT YOU DO THE SAME.

WE MOSTLY DRAW SHADOWS WITH THE SUN DIRECTLY BEHIND AND ABOVE THE STATION POINT OR VIEWER. WITH THE SUN IN THIS POSITION SHADE AND SHADOW ARE DISTRIBUTED MORE EVENLY OVER THE BUILDING. IF THE SUN IS TO THE RIGHT OR LEFT OF THE BUILDING, ONE SIDE WILL BE IN SHADE WHICH SOMETIMES MAY CREATE MORE DRAMA BUT THE SHADED SIDE WILL SHOW LESS DETAIL. SOME EXAMPLES OF SUN POSITION ARE ON THE OPPOSITE PAGE.

LET US NOT FORGET SHADOWS CAST BY ELEMENTS OF THE ENTOURAGE. WE CANNOT STRESS ENOUGH THE IMPORTANCE OF SHADE AND SHADOW AS A KEY ELEMENT IN DESCRIBING THE FORM AND DEPTH IN YOUR BUILDING AND ITS ENVIRONMENT.

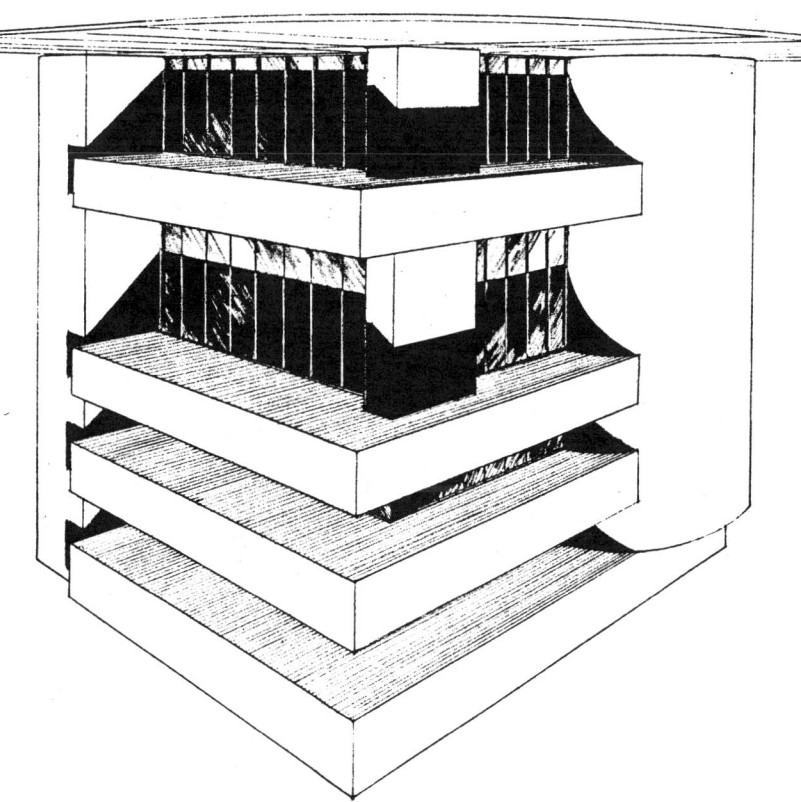
SUN BEHIND VIEWER

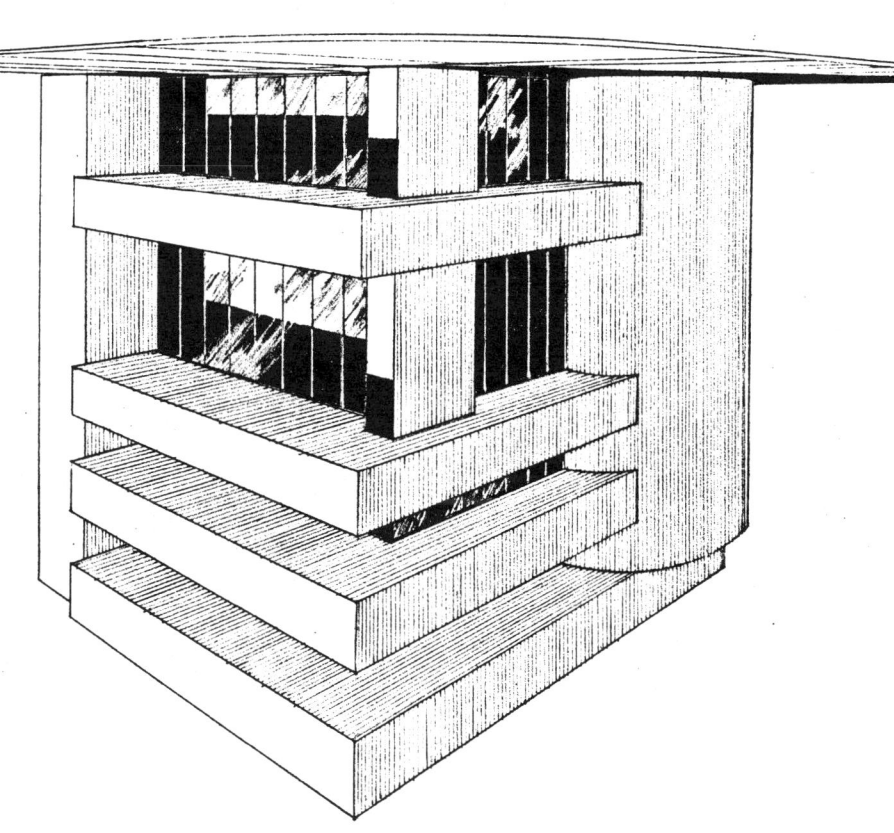
SUN TO THE RIGHT OF VIEWER

site plans and elevations

site plan and elevation embellishment

EVERY ARCHITECT AND DESIGNER KNOWS HOW TO DRAW SITE PLANS AND ELEVATIONS. THE TRICK HERE IS TO TAKE FLAT BUILDING ELEVATIONS AND SITE PLANS AND BY ADDING SHADE, SHADOW AND ENTOURAGE CREATE A PICTURE THE LAYMAN UNDERSTANDS. SHADE AND SHADOW ON THE BUILDINGS GIVE THEM 3 DIMENSIONS, ADDING FOREGROUND AND BACKGROUND ADDS DEPTH AND CONTEXT, THUS GIVING YOUR FLAT BUILDING A FEELING OF REALITY.

IN DRAWING EXTERIOR ELEVATIONS, USE A PRINT OR TRACING PAPER AS AN OVERLAY AND POSITION TREES, CARS AND PEOPLE SO THAT THEY FOLLOW THE LANDSCAPING AND PARKING PLAN; SOME TREES MIGHT BE LEFT OUT SO THAT THE BUILDING IS NOT TOTALLY COVERED, OR MAYBE SHOW TREES IN THE FALL STATE. PARKING LOTS SHOULD NOT BE SHOWN FULL TRY 40 TO 50% OCCUPIED. PEOPLE SHOULD BE USED TO SHOW SCALE AND ADD LIFE TO YOUR DRAWING. IN MOST CASES, TWO OR THREE ARE SUFFICIENT. THE NEXT STAGE OF DEVELOPMENT IS TO ESTABLISH THE DIRECTION OF SUNLIGHT. ONCE AGAIN USE A PRINT OR OVERLAY PAPER AND TRY A FEW SKETCHES; BE BOLD AND LET THE SHADOWS MAKE A REAL STATEMENT. WE HAVE FOUND MOST TIMES THE SUN STRIKING THE BUILDING AT A 45° ANGLE WORKS BEST.

WE BASICALLY FOLLOW THE SAME PROCESS IN RENDERING OUR SITE PLANS. AGAIN OUR GOAL IS TO CREATE DEPTH AND DIMENSION TO AN OTHERWISE FLAT DRAWING. FOLLOWING AN EXISTING OR PROPOSED LANDSCAPE PLAN USE THE TREES DRAWN FROM ABOVE IN THE TRACING FILE; ENLARGE OR REDUCE THEM TO FIT THE SCALE OF YOUR PLAN. SHOW CARS AS REQUIRED AND JUMP IN WITH THAT BOLD SHADOW - YOU WILL FIND SUGGESTIONS FOR DRAWING GROUND COVER, WATER AND OTHER MATERIALS FROM A PLAN VIEW IN THE NATURAL TEXTURES SECTION OF THIS BOOK.

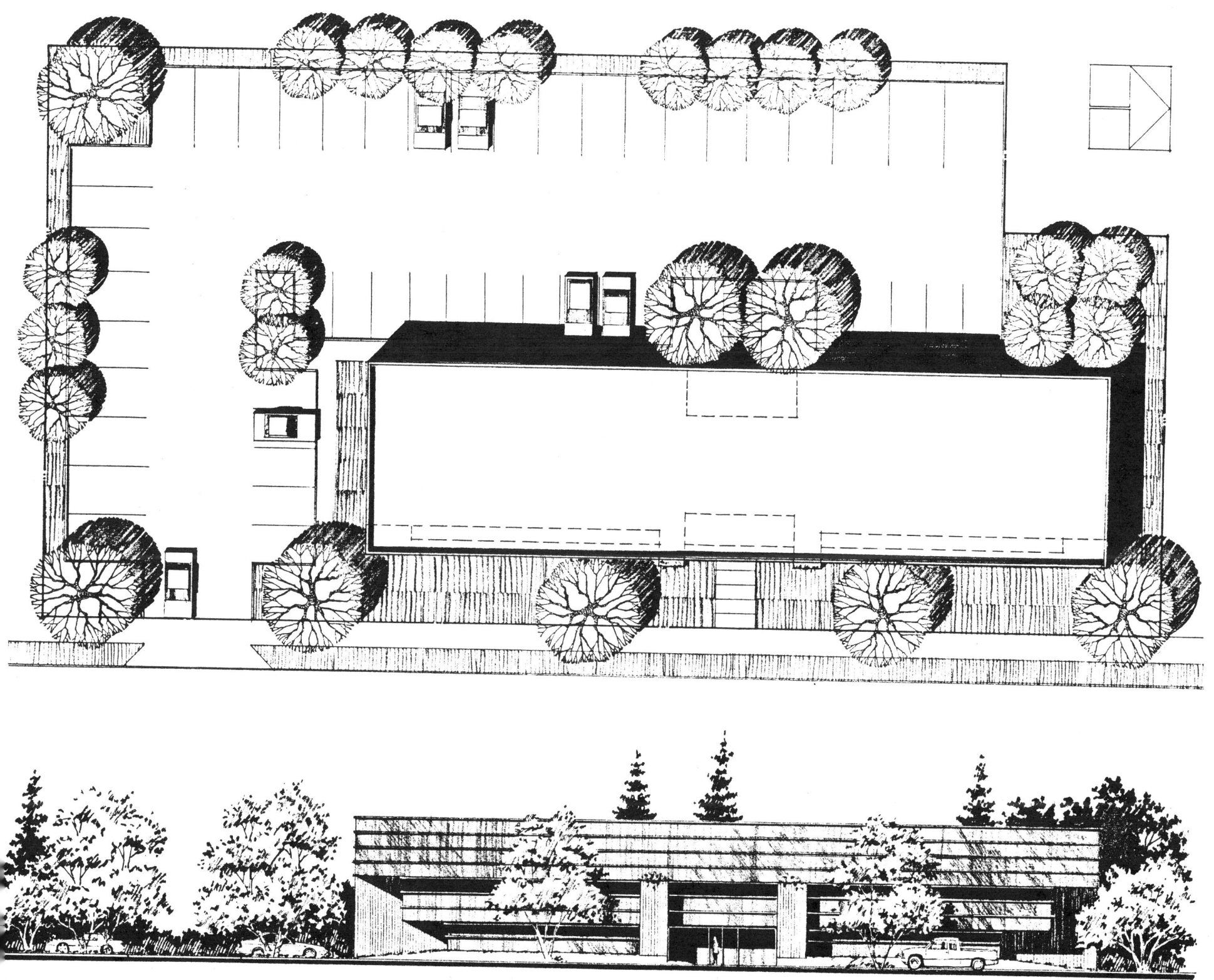

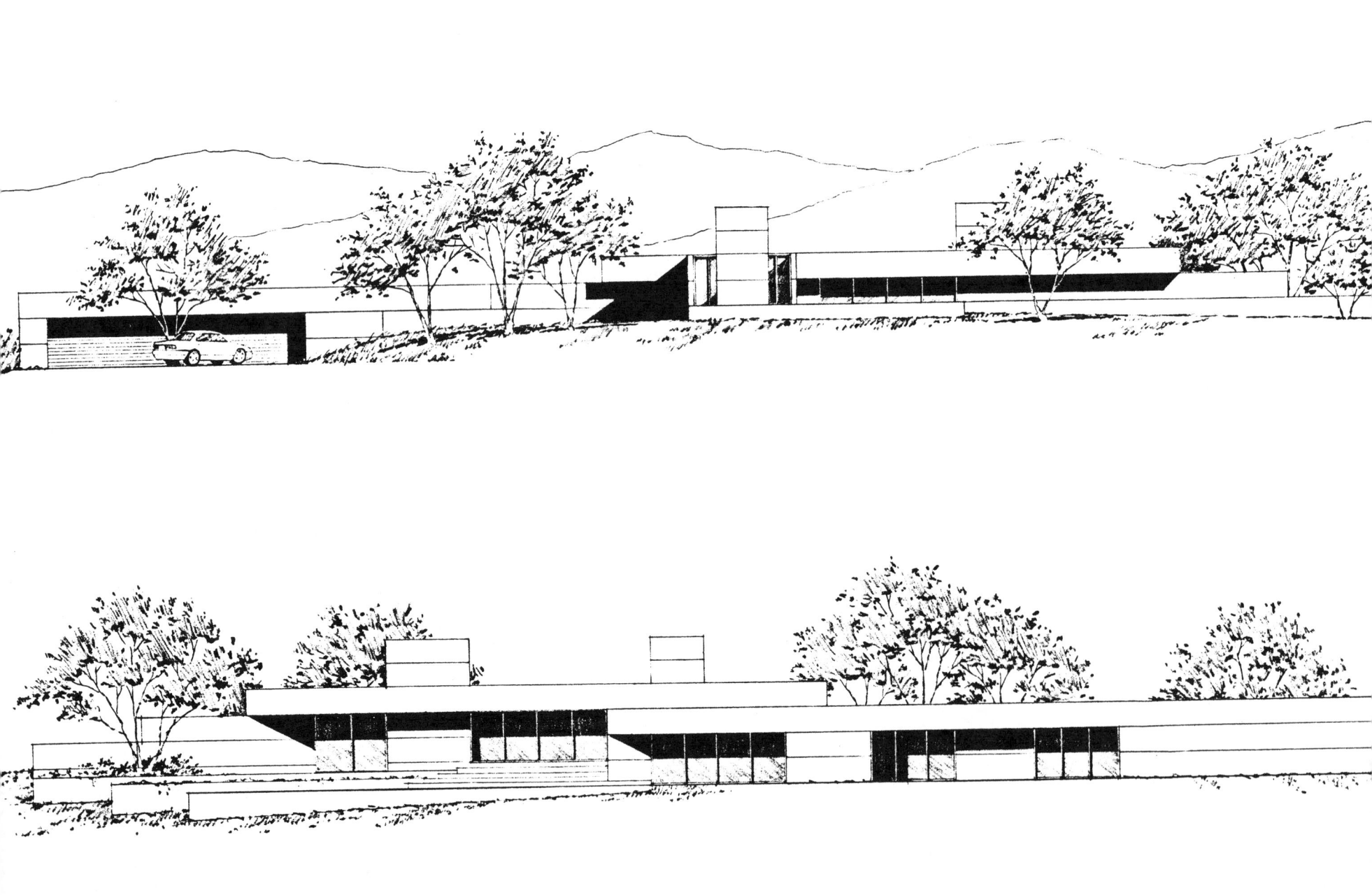

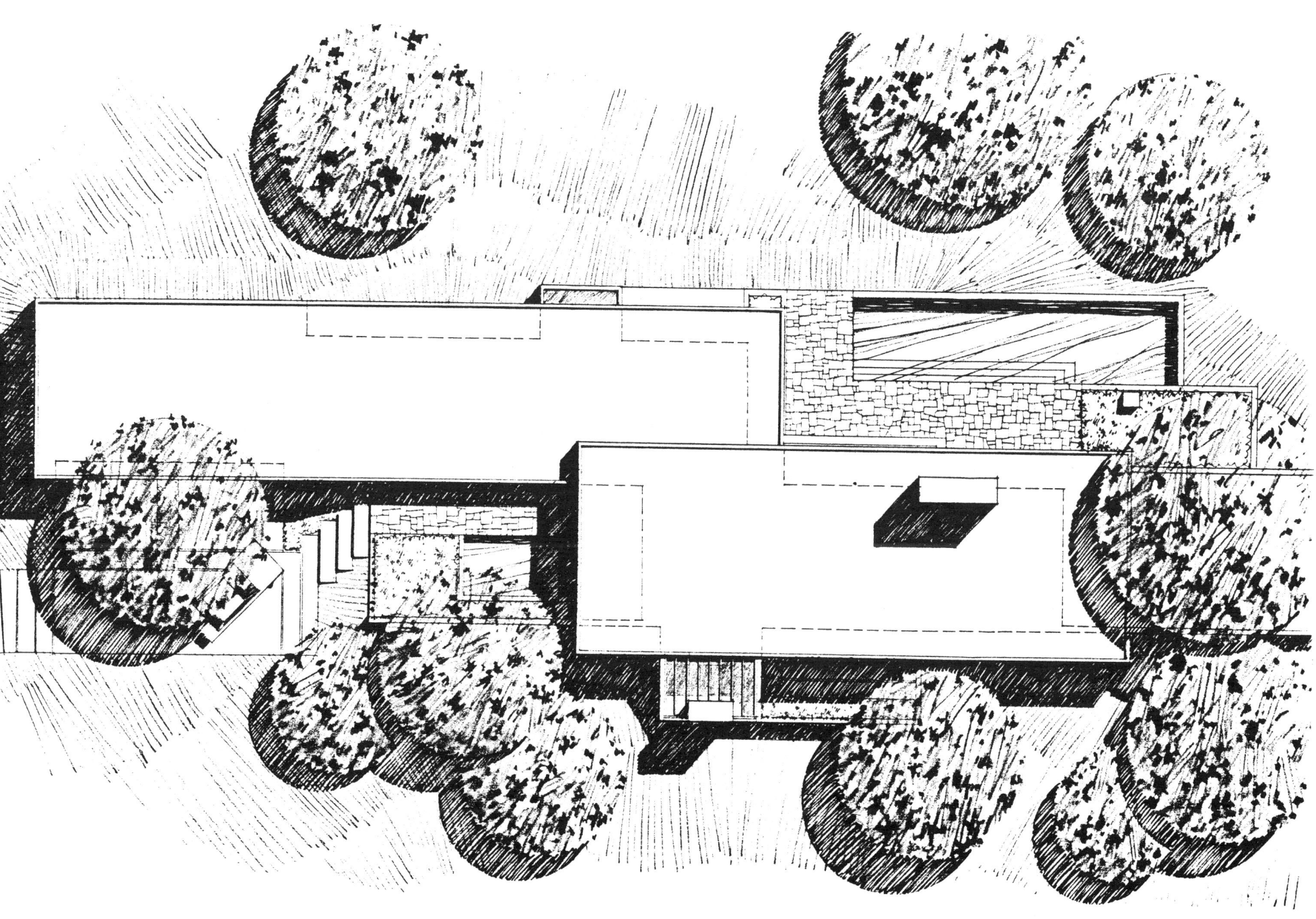

TRACING FILE

vegetation

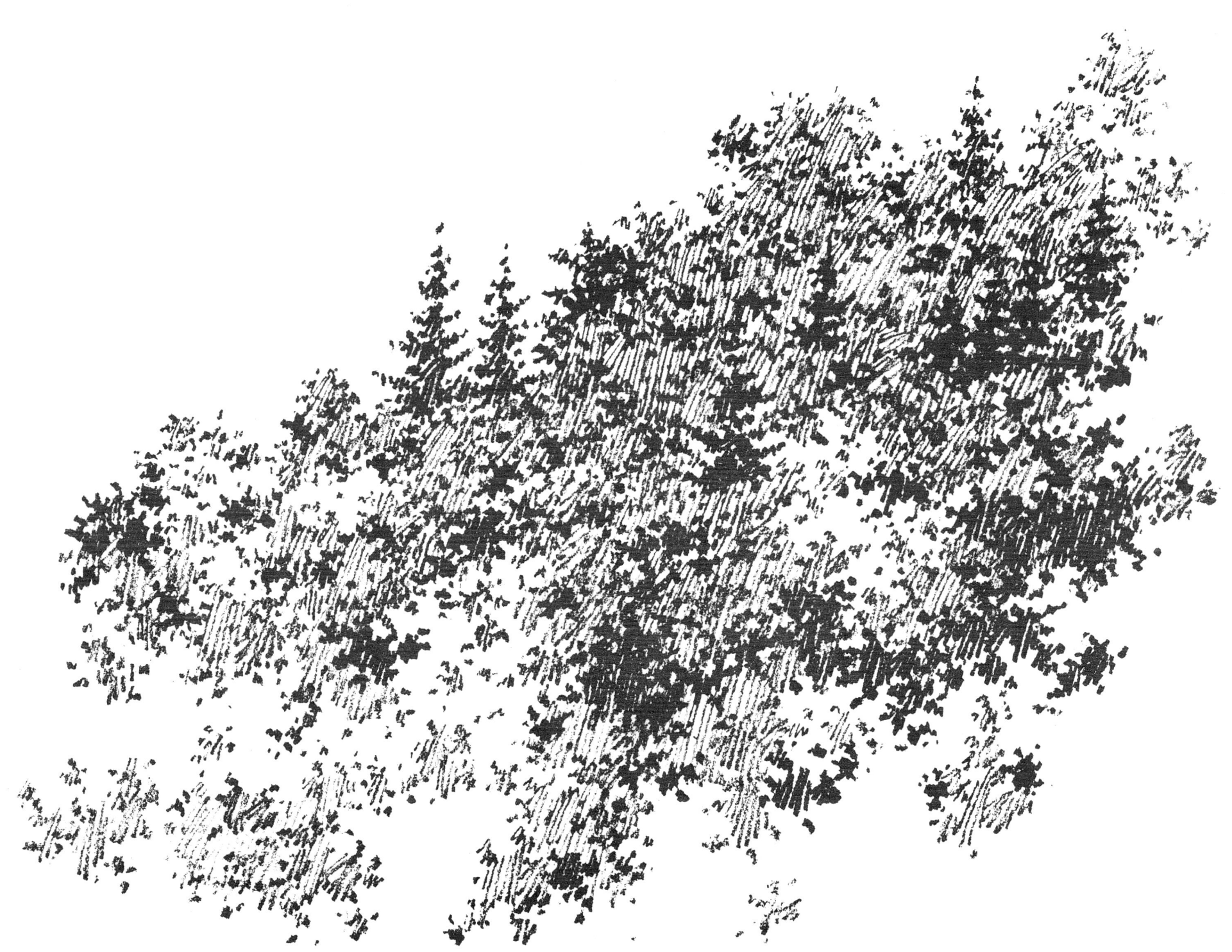

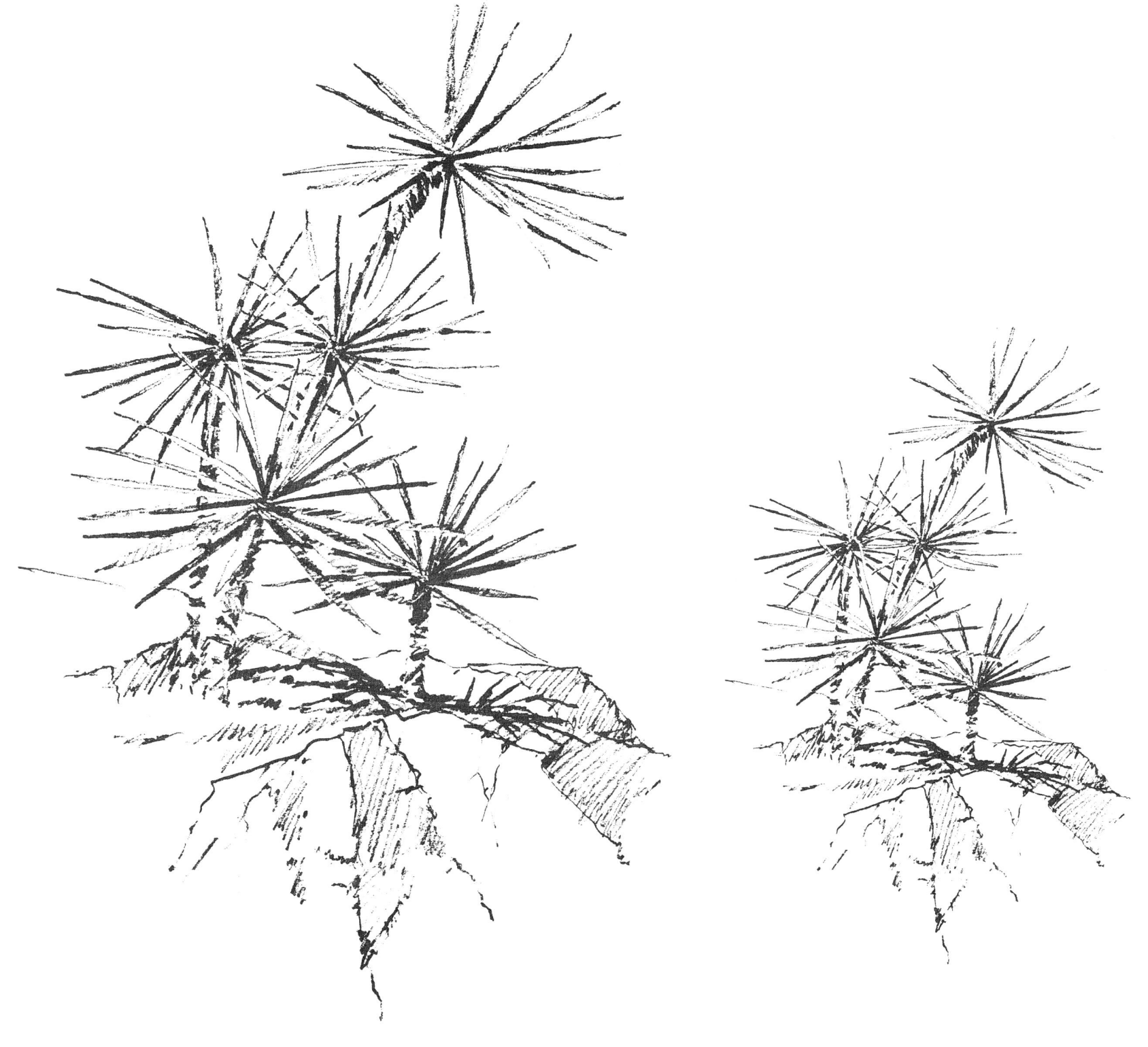

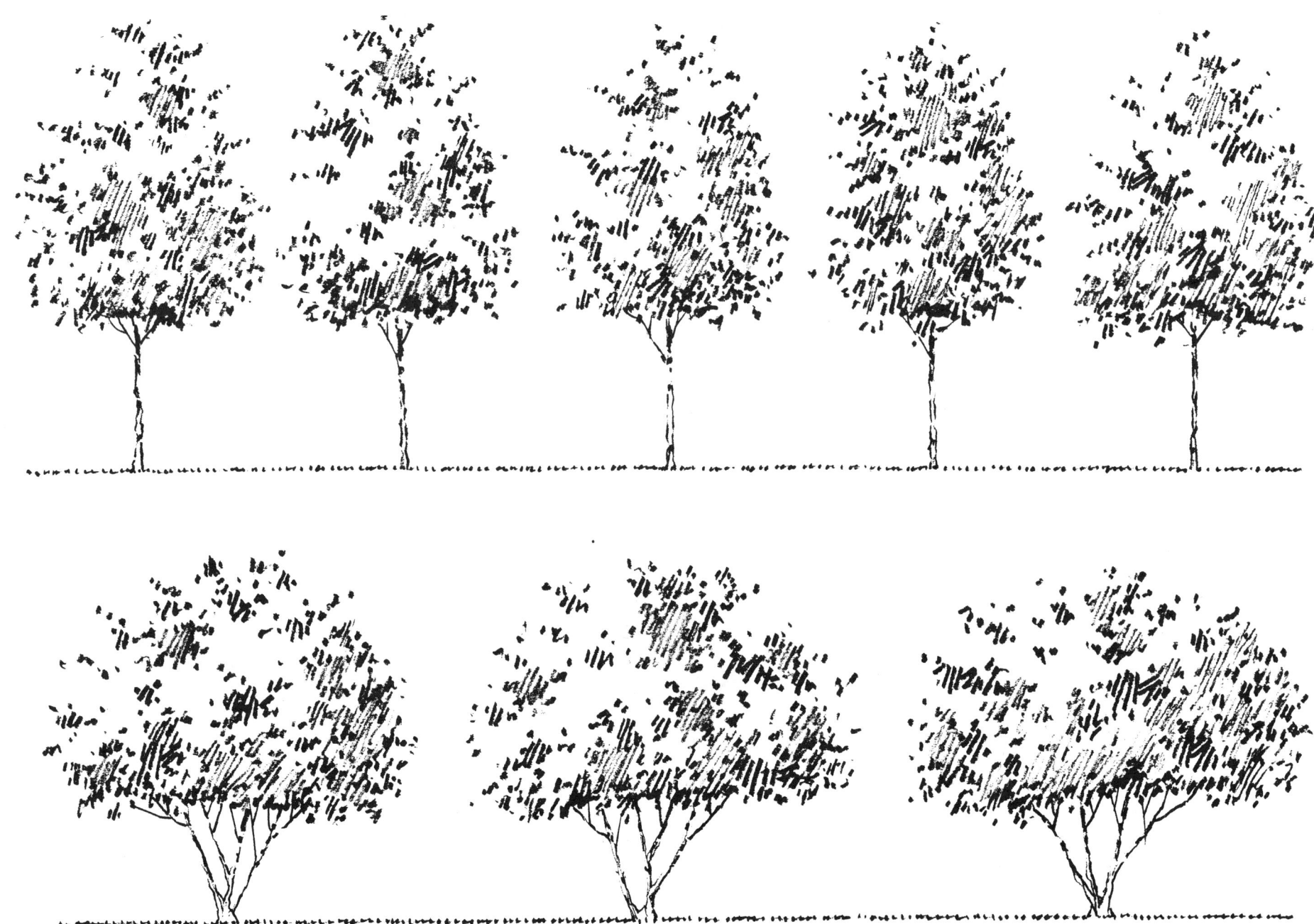

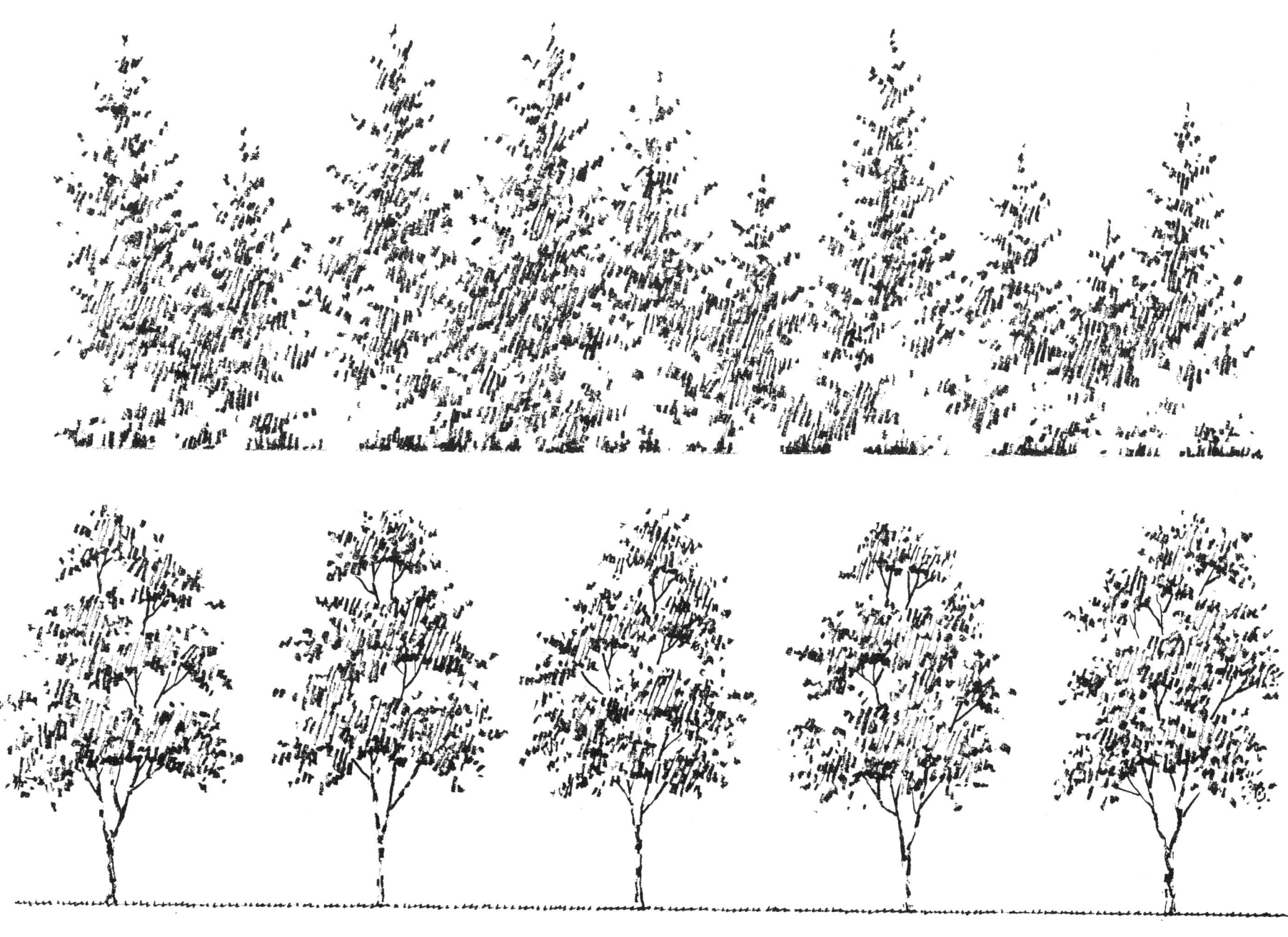

121

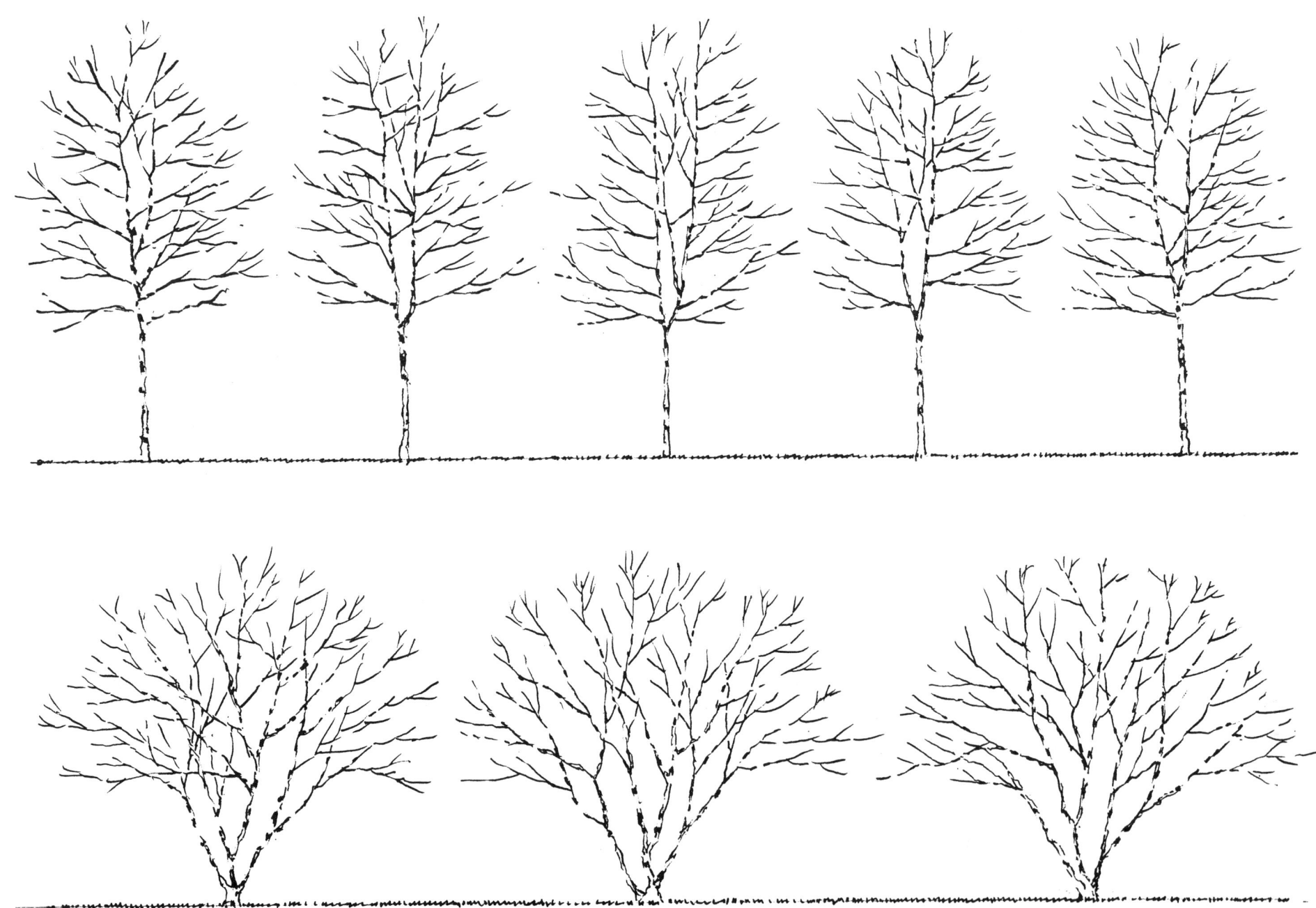

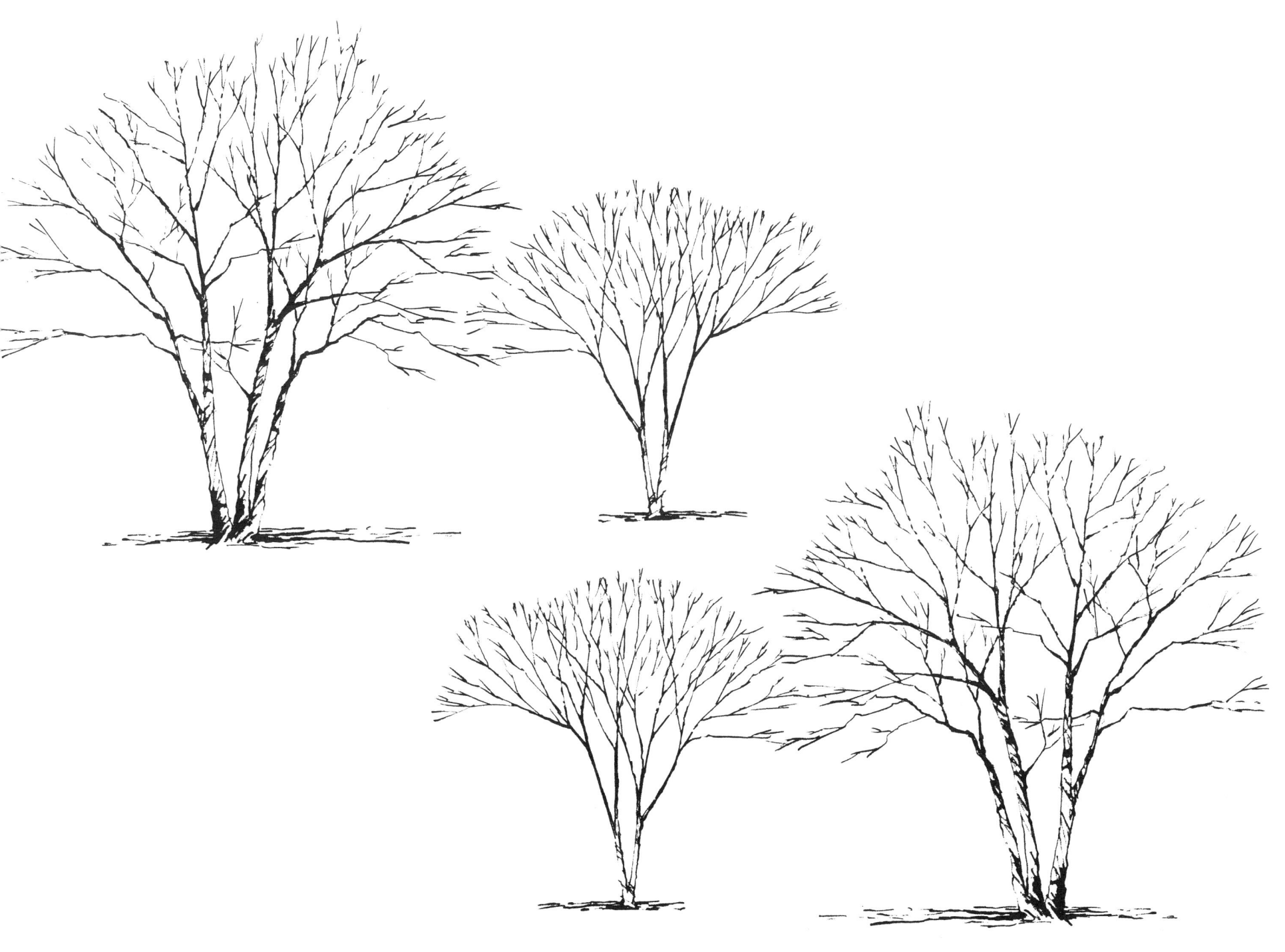

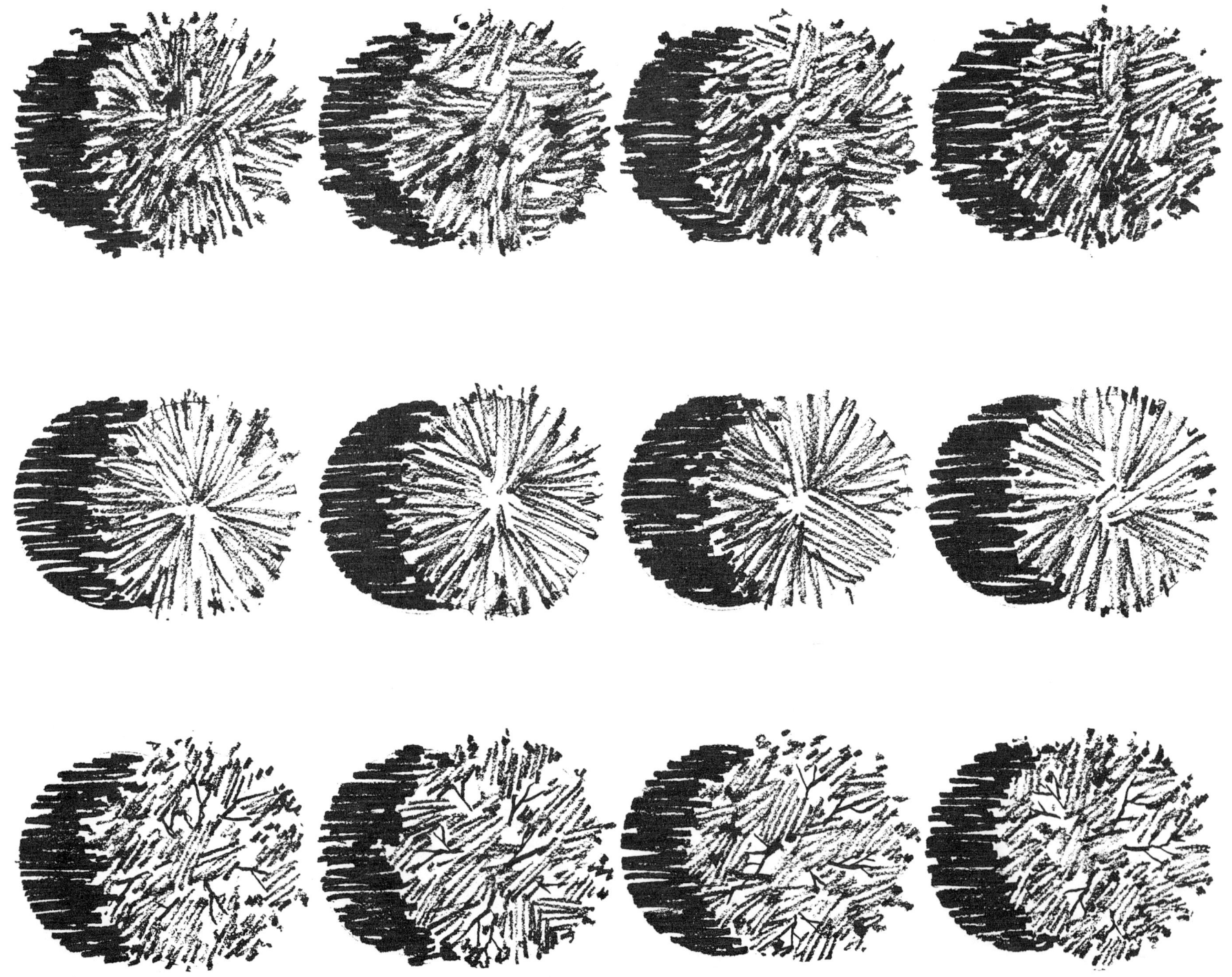

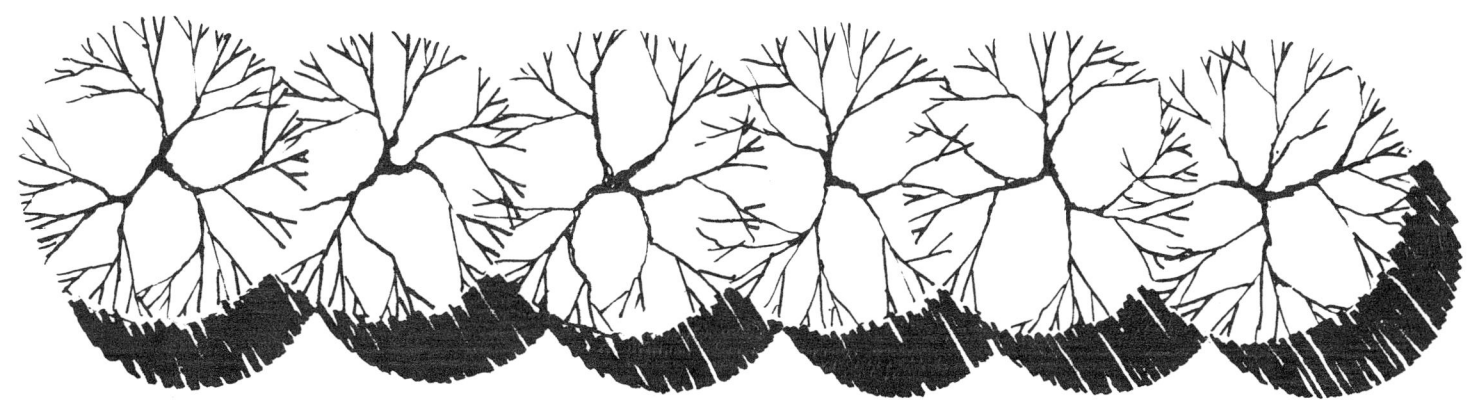

127

vehicles

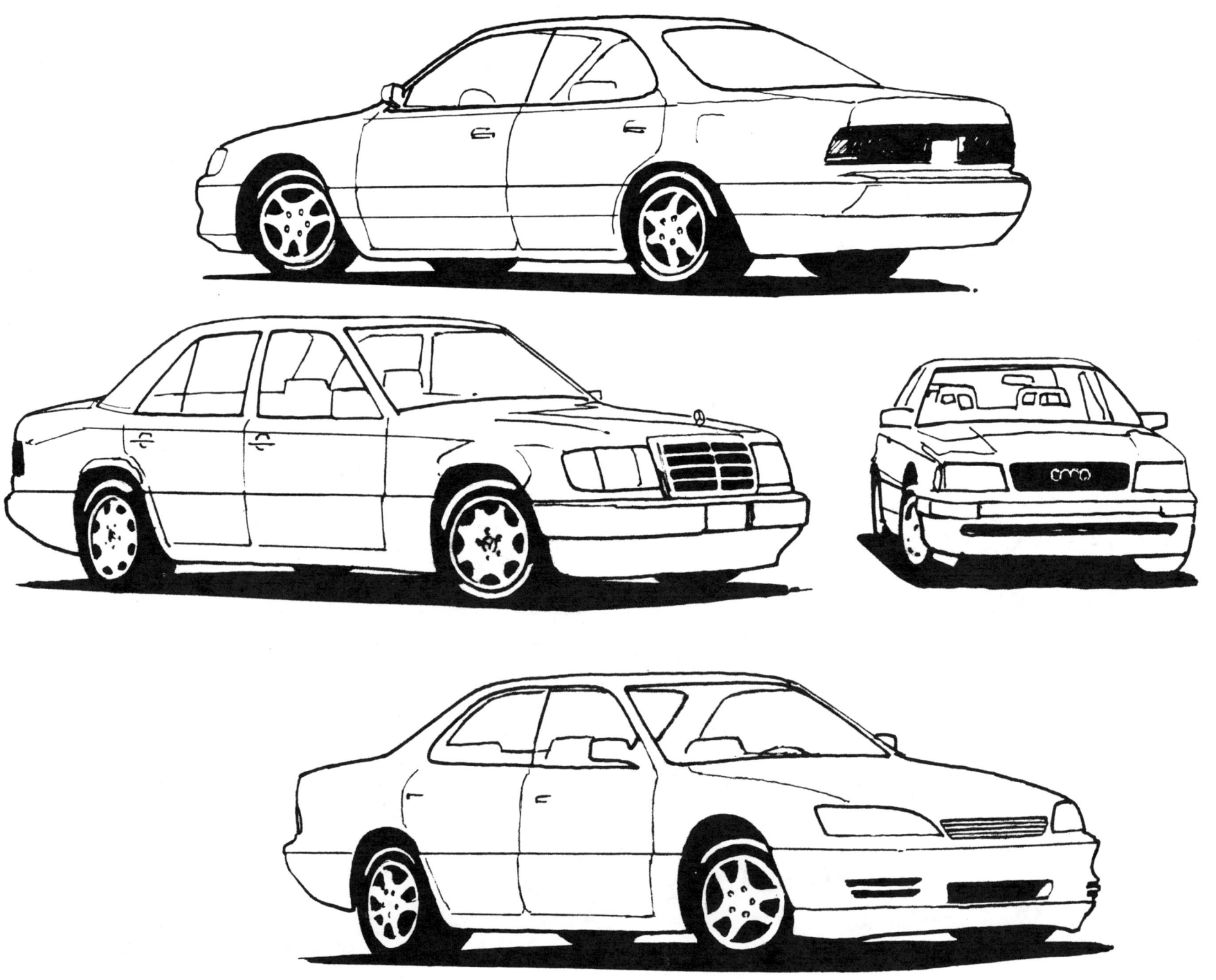

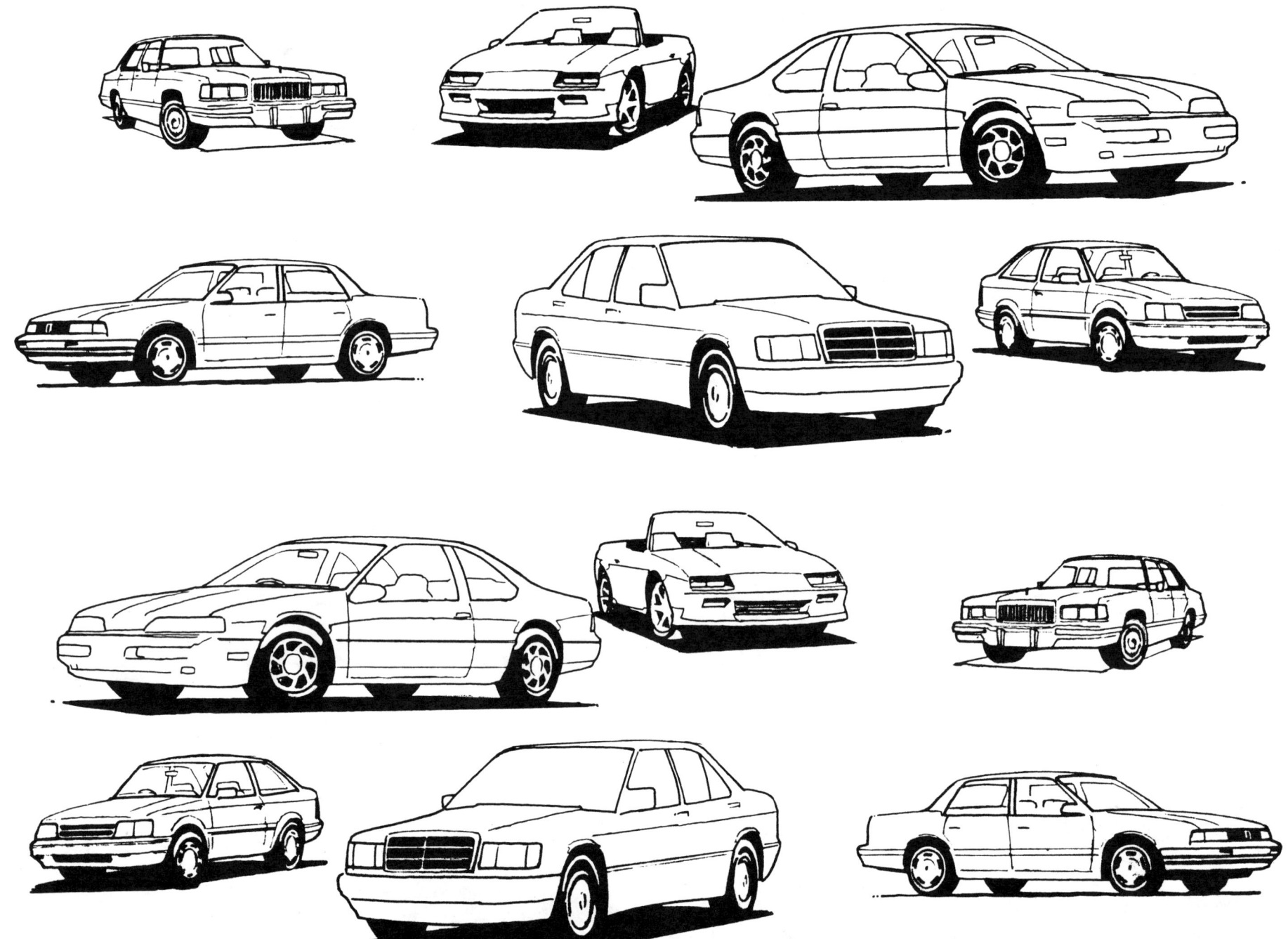

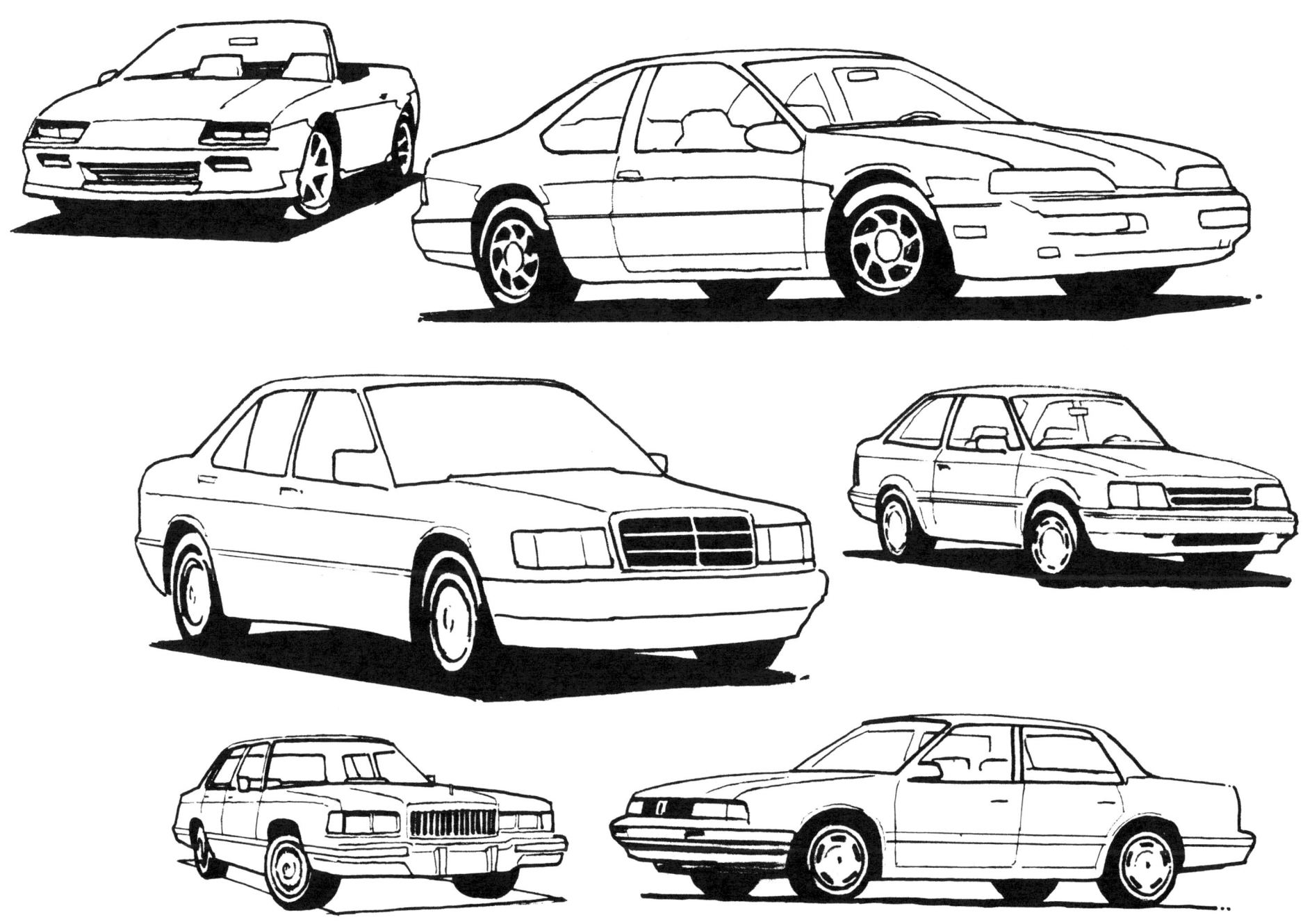

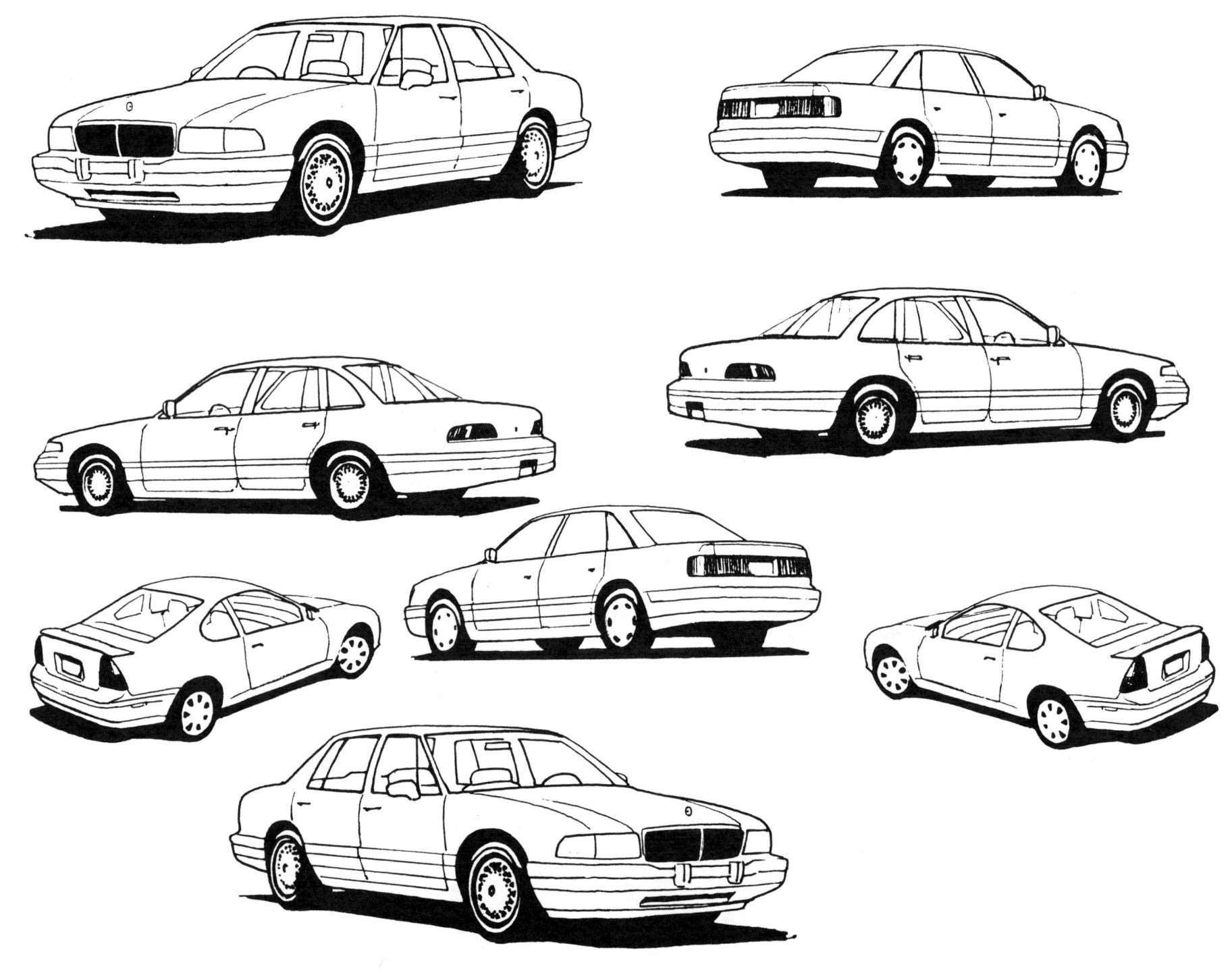

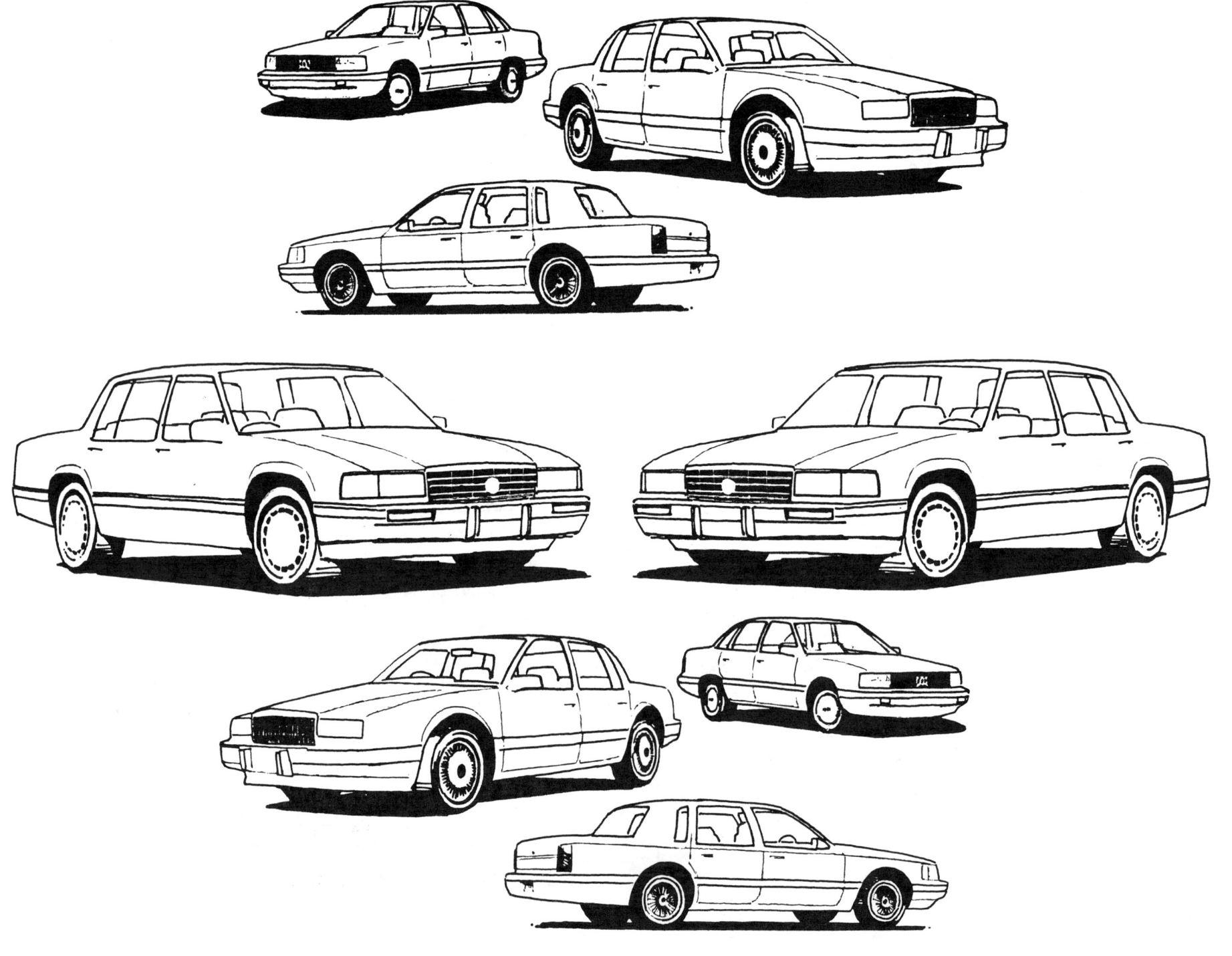

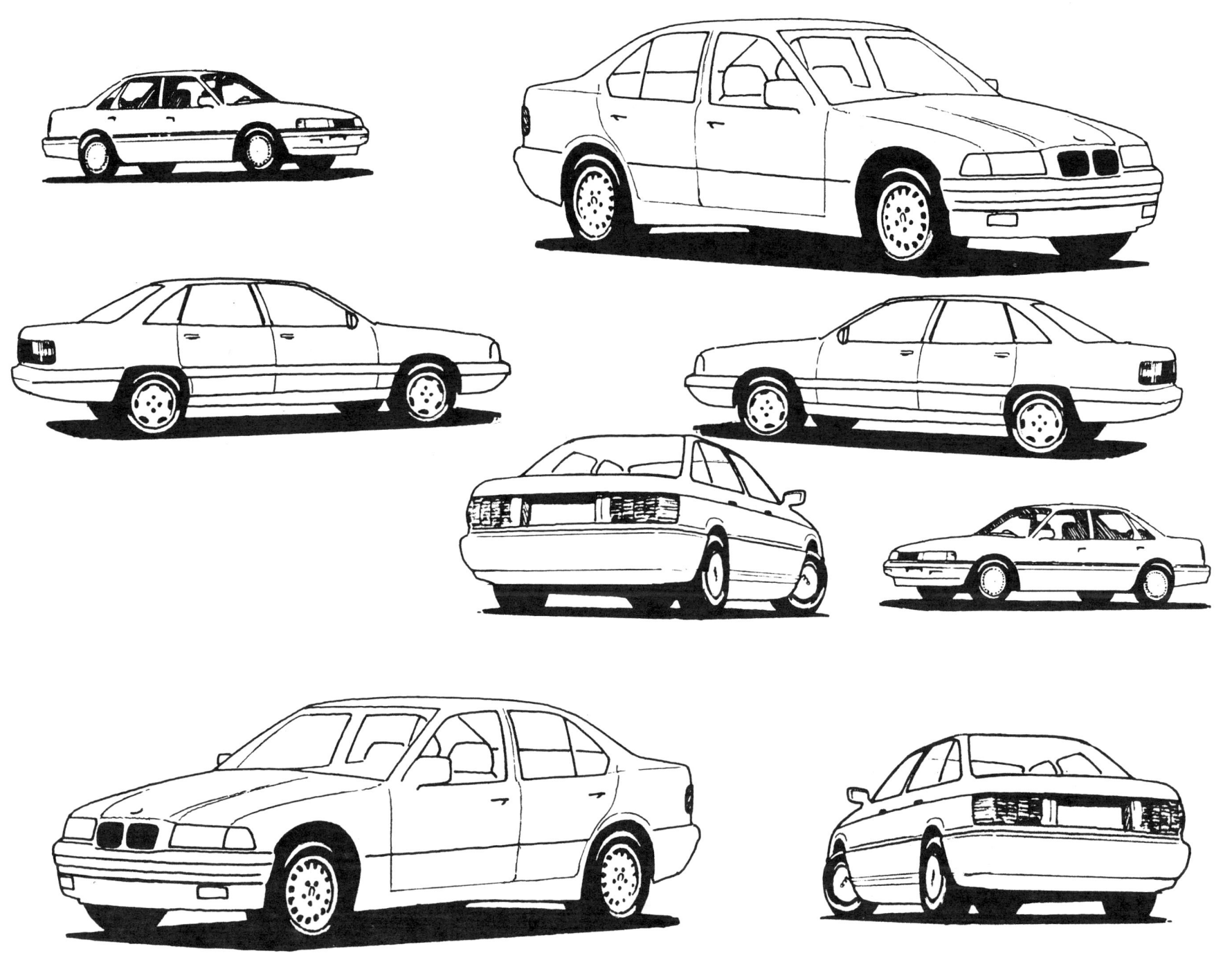

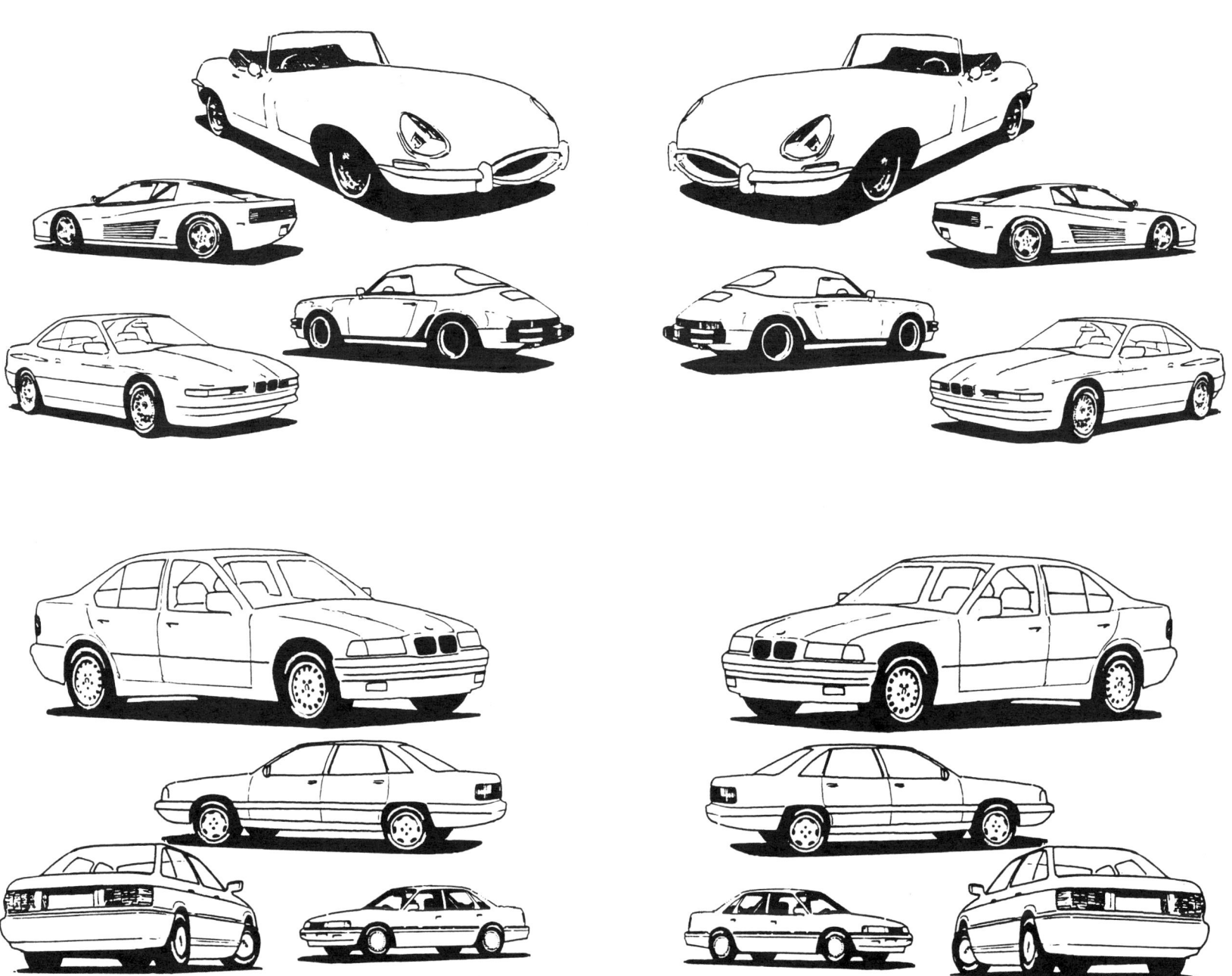

167

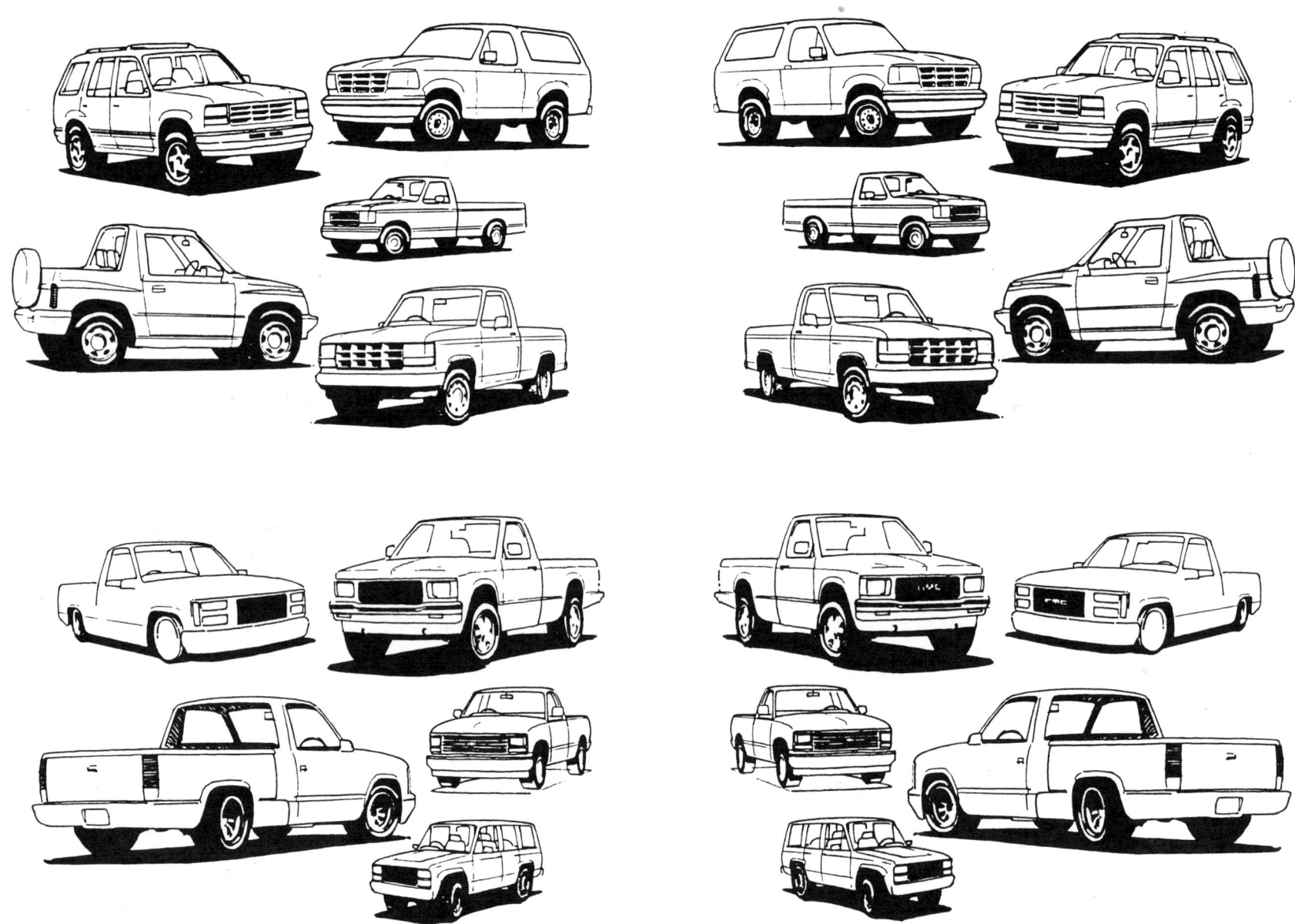

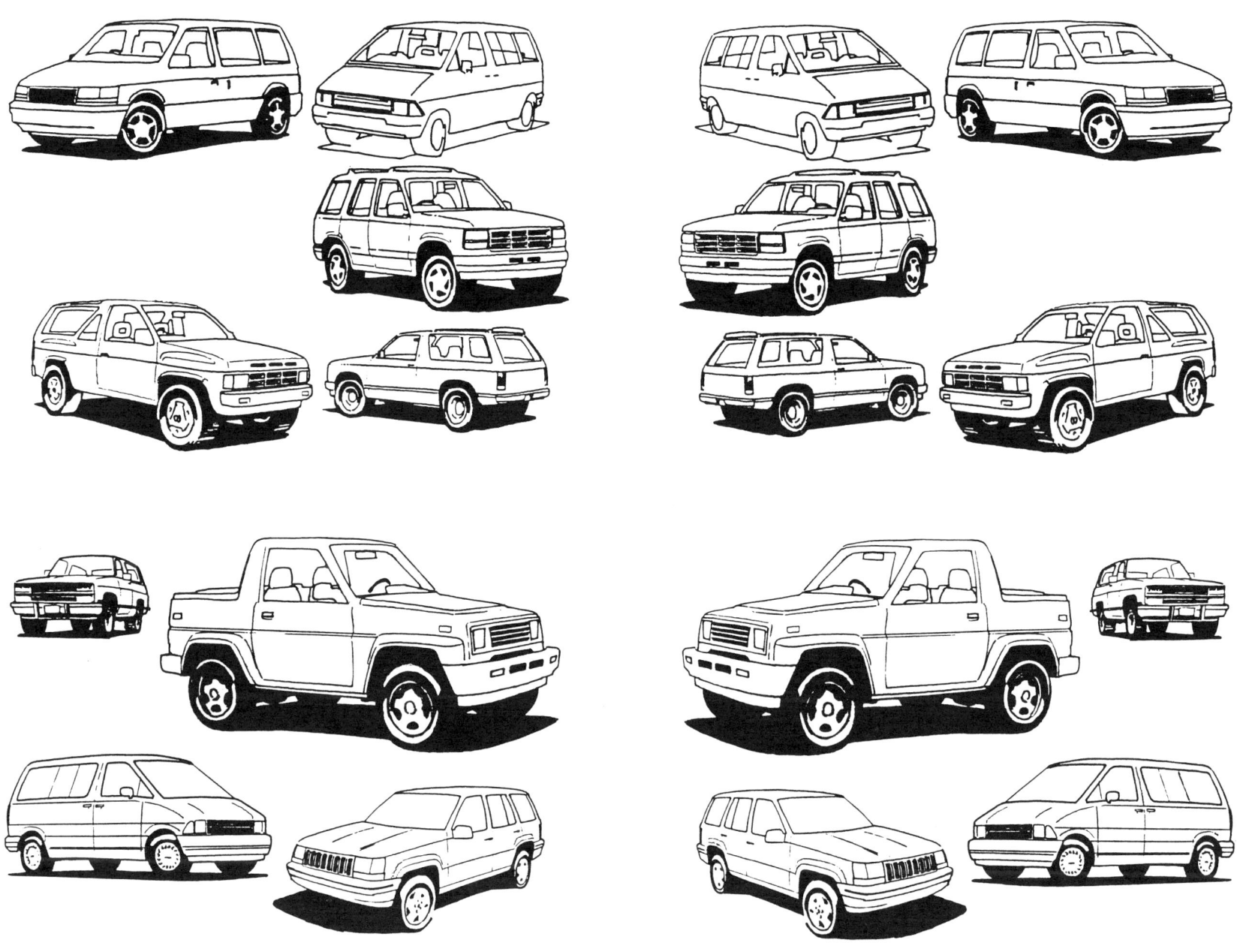

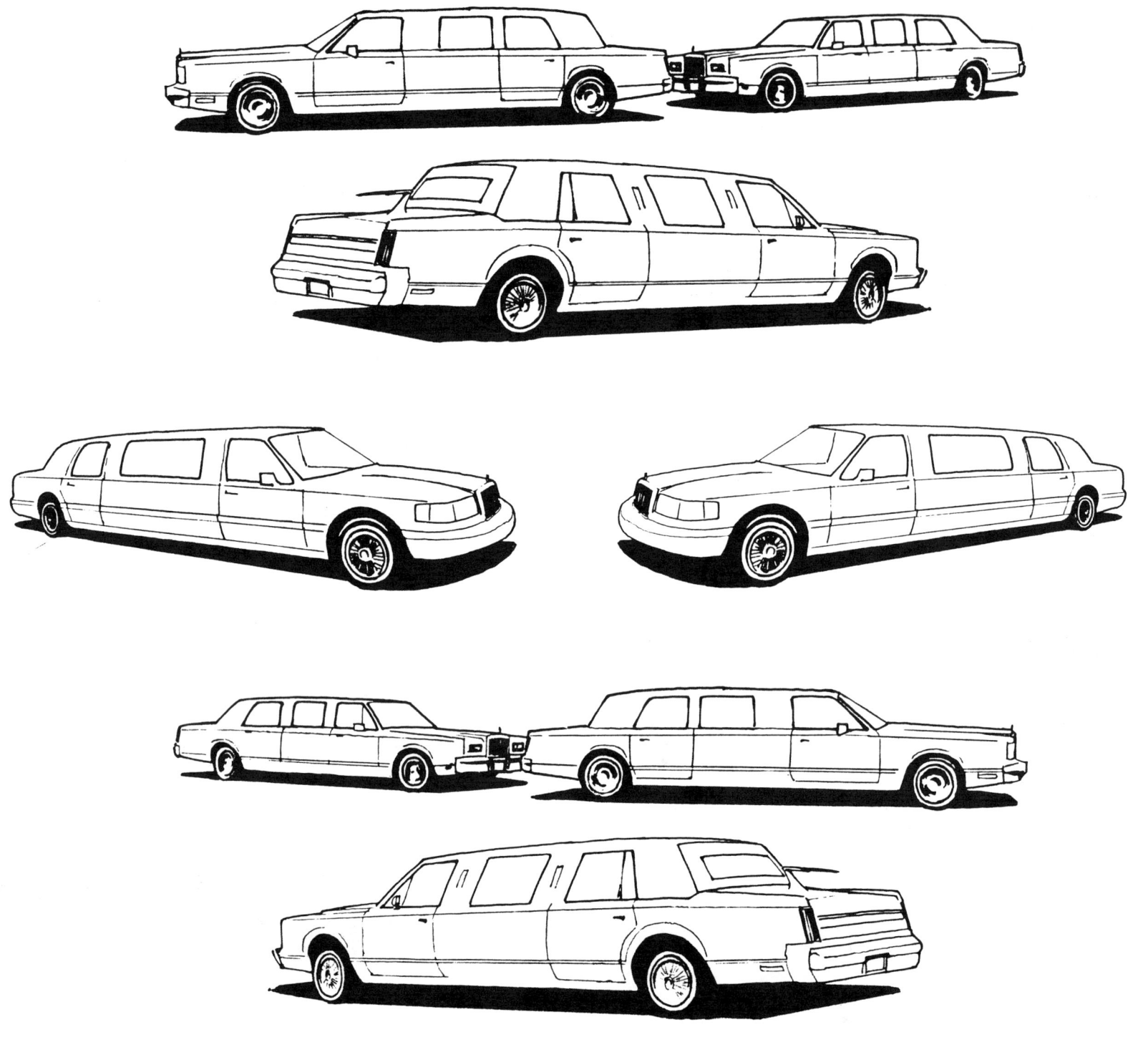

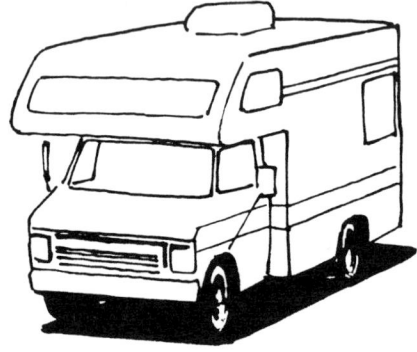

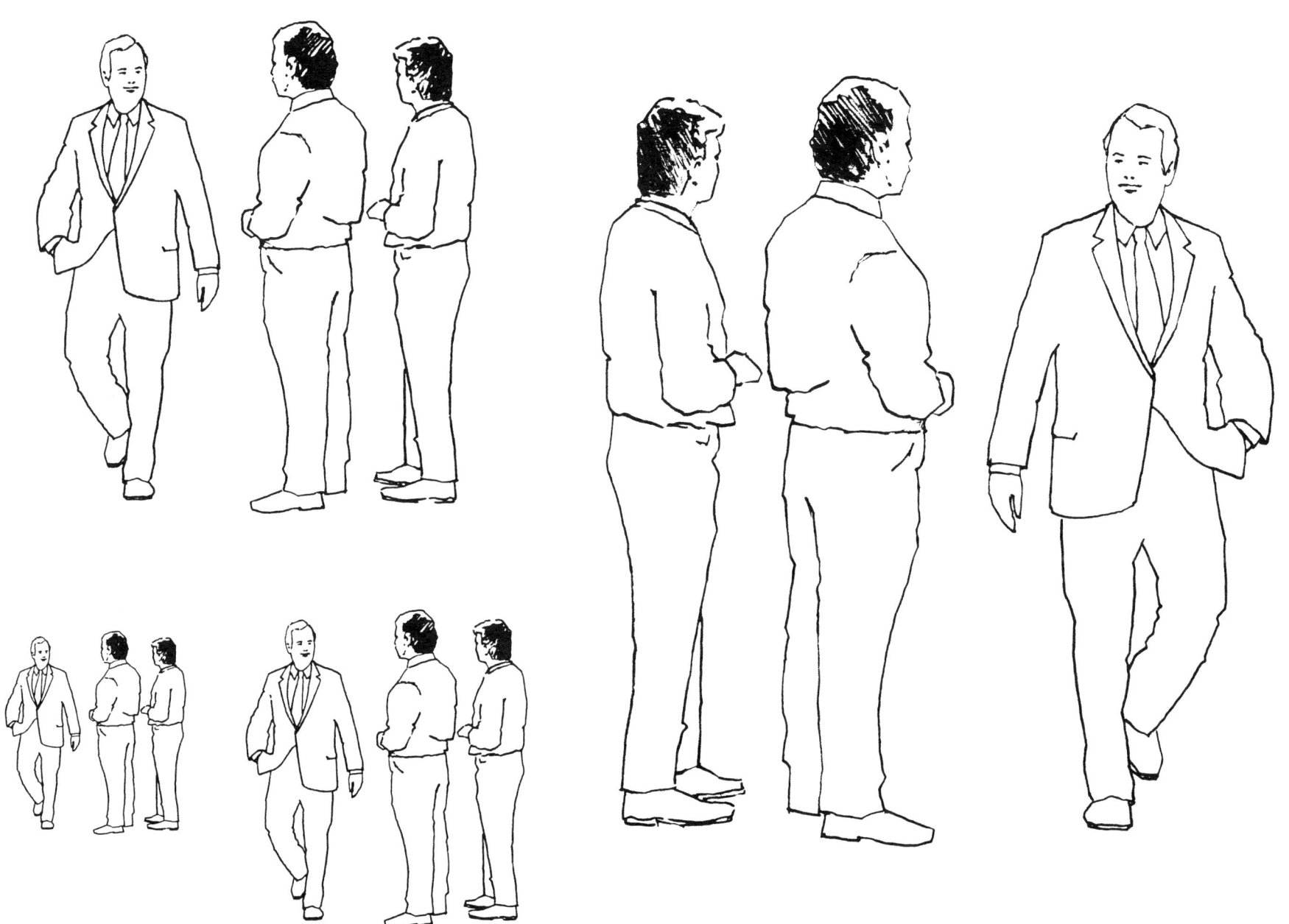

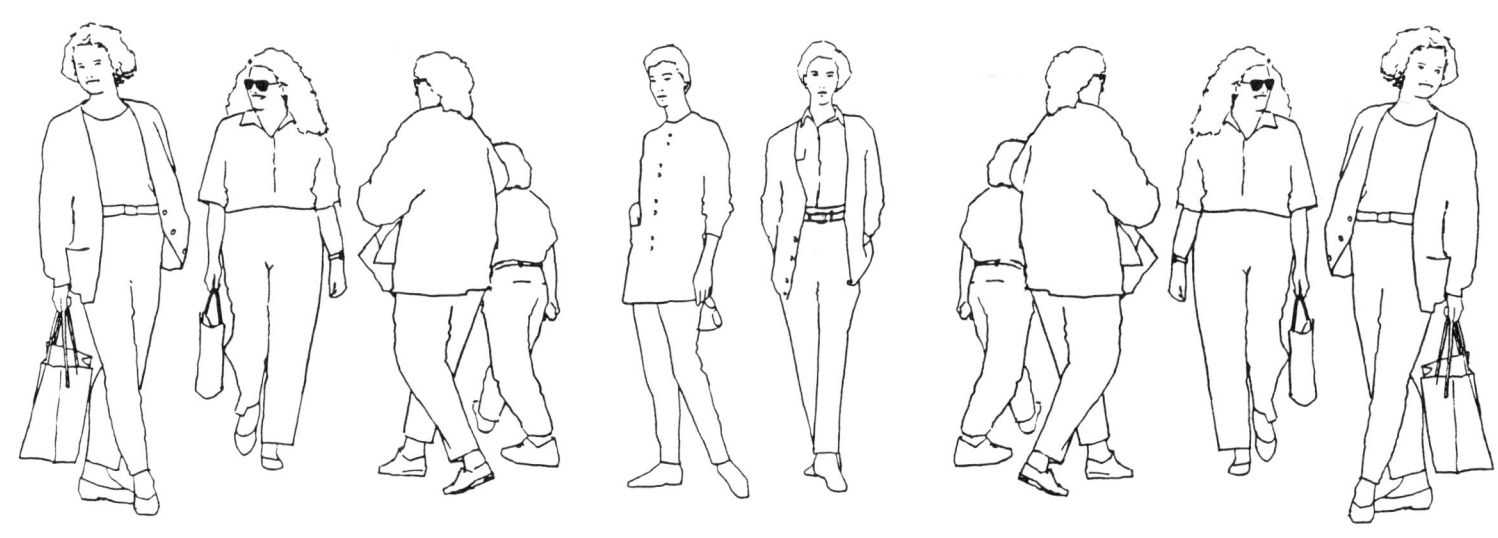

221

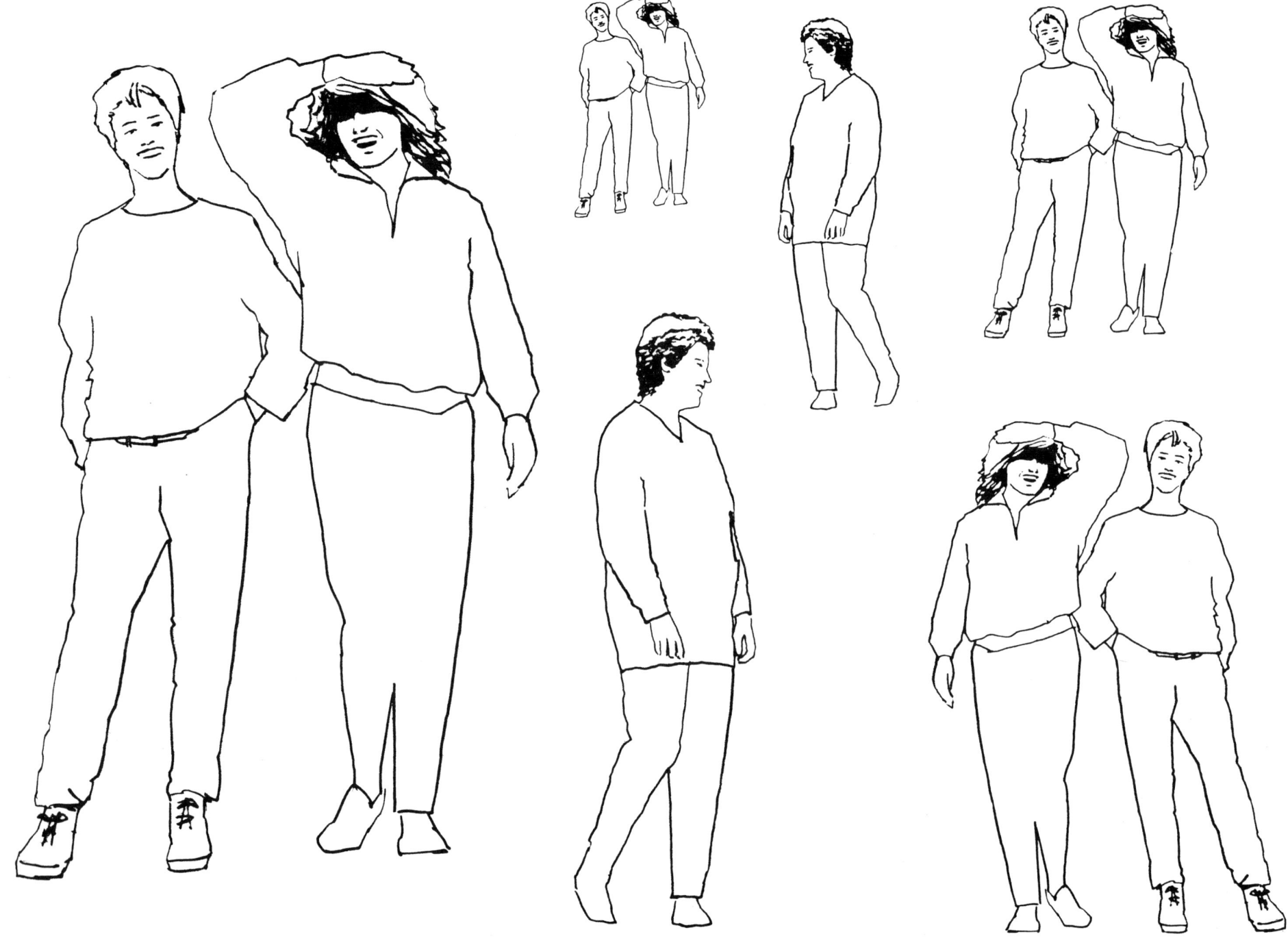

233

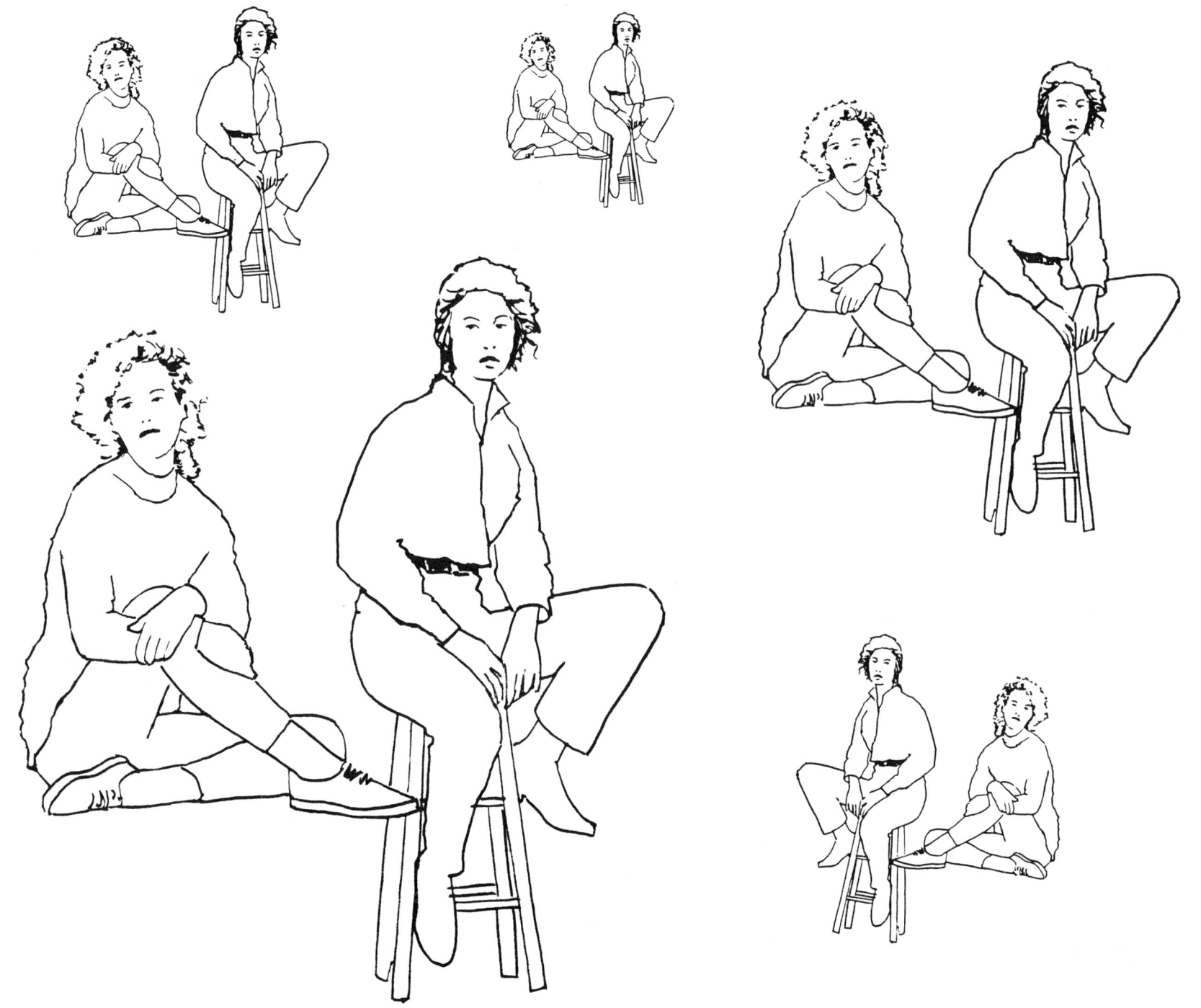

the authors

SEVEN YEARS AGO, GARY TOBEY AND NELS HILDETON STARTED DESIGN CONCEPTS, AN ARCHITECTURAL ILLUSTRATION FIRM LOCATED IN SANTA ROSA, CALIFORNIA, WHICH SPECIALIZES IN CONCEPTUAL DESIGN SERVICES, LAND PLANNING, AND ARCHITECTURAL RENDERING. THEY HAVE WORKED TOGETHER WITH ARCHITECTS THROUGHOUT THE COUNTRY TO PROVIDE EXCEPTIONAL PRESENTATION PACKAGES FOR THE DESIGN COMMUNITY.

AS AN ARCHITECT AND ILLUSTRATOR, NELS HAS BEEN PRACTICING IN THE ARCHITECTURAL PROFESSION FOR THIRTY YEARS AND HAS TAUGHT ARCHITECTURAL DELINEATION AT THE COLLEGE LEVEL FOR SEVERAL YEARS. GARY HAS TWENTY TWO YEARS OF EXPERIENCE AS AN ARCHITECTURAL DESIGNER AND DELINEATOR AND HAS RECEIVED NUMEROUS AWARDS FOR DESIGN.